What's Wrong With Sex Education?

Melvin Anchell, M.D., A.S.P.P., N.A.A.P.
©1991

Illustrations by Lisa George

Additional Illustrations
from *Killers of Children*

DEDICATED TO

The Hoffman Center
for the Family
in Memory of Kathryn P. Hoffman
and Daniel R. Hoffman

FOR

decent people — loving people in our Nation, who, in an environ-ment gone mad with unbridled physical sex, exemplify the life sustaining nature of human sexuality.

By example they teach their children the wonder of sexually fulfilled man/woman monogamous love — the meaning of life itself.

ISBN 0-9630040-0-X

Published in the United States
by The Hoffman Center
for The Family
5266 Citizens Parkway
Selma, AL 36701

Table of Contents

SECTION I

SEX EDUCATION

A. THE FACTS OF HUMAN SEXUALITY

Public school sex education programs have been established throughout the United States for over two decades.

Before discussing these programs and **the harm they cause students and society**, three basic psychoanalytical facts concerning human sexuality should be mentioned. These three truths are inherent, and they apply to all people throughout the world.

1. The first established truth is that in humans, "sex is an intimate affair"...two people in love seek total privacy during their sexual intimacies. Intrusions of others into their physical sexual life normally arouse feelings of shame and intense jealousy in both men and women.

> "Jealousy is one of those affective states, like grief, that may be described as normal. If anyone appears to be without it, the inference is justified that it has undergone severe repression and consequently plays all the greater part in his unconscious mental life.
>
> "...normal jealousy is compounded of grief, the pain caused by the thought of losing the loved object and...of feelings of enmity against the successful rival and...of some self criticism which tries to hold the person himself accountable for his loss."
>
> *Sexuality and the Psychology of Love*
> — by Sigmund Freud

The more two people are in love, the more they suffice for each

other. It is only when love is lacking that people are able to share physical sex with a series of partners or in groups. When this takes place, a regression occurs to a primitive state in which love plays no part in the sex act.

To repeat, the first fact is, intimate sexual love is an inborn characteristic of human sexuality. Its need to be limited to two people only is prescribed by the very nature of the sex act itself.

Today's public school sex programs disregard this initial fact concerning human sexuality. In all sex classes — coeducational or otherwise — students are desensitized to the intimate nature of physical sex, if only for the reason that to discuss sex, students must openly express their innermost sexual feelings and at the same time become involved with similar sexual thoughts of fellow classmates.

In short, it is not possible to publicly discuss sex in school classes without damaging the vitally intimate nature of sex.

2. The second psychoanalytic fact is that in humans, the sexual instinct is composed of two currents — an affectionate current and a physical current. The affectionate component is as important — if not more so — than the physical component.

For human sexuality to be complete, there must be a confluence, a coming together, of the affectionate and physical components of sex. When affectionate needs are weakened and physical sex is all that remains, *sex becomes meaningless and life becomes empty.*

Throughout public school sex classrooms, physical aspects of sex are emphasized, while affectionate needs are damned by faint praise.

> "To believe that psychoanalysis seeks a cure for neurotic disorders by giving a free rein to sexuality is a serious misunderstanding which can only be justified by ignorance."
>
> *Psychoanalysis*
> — by Sigmund Freud

The emphasis on teaching physical sex is necessarily so — not because of possible shortcomings in a sex teacher — but because physical sex is *ALL* that can be taught in a sex class. There is nothing more. Affectionate, tender feelings for a sex partner and tenderness in loving cannot be learned from a school textbook.

And, the fact is that the very teaching of physical sex publicly coarsens and severely diminishes the affectionate nature of human sexuality.

3. The third basic fact is that in humans, unlike any other creature, three phases of sexual development occur before adult sexual maturity is reached. The first phase begins at birth and lasts through the 5th year of life. The second phase of human sexual development occurs between the ages of 6 and 12. And the third stage of sexual development starts around the age of 13 and continues into early adulthood.

> Vann Spruniell, M.D. (Psychoanalyst, Associate Professor of Psychiatry, Tulane University), in an article, "Don't Force Grownup Sex Education on Children," *Medical Economics Magazine,* December 6, 1971:
>
> "Dr. Warren J. Gadpaille [American Association of Sex Educators and Counselors and Consultant on Family Living Programs]...would provide, from kindergarten through high school, information about anatomy, 'dirty' words, procreation, sexual attitudes and sexual practices. All this would be derived from small-animal demonstrations and a series of 'frank discussions.'
>
> "What of respected scientific opinion that sex education might be 'too much, too soon?' "

Today's public school sex education — which, incidentally, Planned Parenthood, a chief school sex education proponent, now euphemistically refers to as "Family Life or Health Programs" — is *not* in accord with natural sexual growth processes occurring in the three phases of human sexual development; thereby making it virtually impossible for sexually educated students to grow into sexually mature adults. There is no school sex program given anywhere at any grade level that does not disrupt normal sexual growth processes.

To understand "why and how" today's Planned Parenthood sponsored sex programs (established in 85% of schools in the United States) cause such irreparable harm to students, let's briefly look at the three phases of human sexual development and, at the same time, also look at the sex teachings given to students during each of these three developmental phases.

B. HUMAN SEXUAL DEVELOPMENT PHASE I

The first phase of human sexual development begins at birth and lasts through the 5th year of life. (It should be noted that the first phase itself is divided into three stages.)

The initial sensual pleasure in life is derived from the sucking that is associated with the infant's need for nourishment. From the very beginning it can be seen that **normal** sensual pleasure is life sustaining.

The sucking — or oral stage — usually comes to an end around the 2nd year of life, at which time the child's main sensual pleasure is then derived from "aggressive-anal" impulses.

Sensual aggressiveness consists of the desire to master another by force rather than by wooing. It may seem strange that the predominant sensual pleasure in a small 2-year old child is derived from aggressiveness, but such pleasure may not seem so surprising if one realizes that cruelty is a primitive vestige that remains a part of the sexual instinct.

The aggressive second stage passes into the third childhood sexual stage at about the age of 3 and continues through the 5th year of life.

During the ages of 3 to 5, the child's primary sensual pleasure is derived from the desire "to see and show nudity." Therefore, from a psychoanalytic standpoint, this stage is exhibitionistic and voyeuristic in nature. It can be readily seen, for example, in the innocent but unmistakable sensual excitement that some 3 to 5

FIRST PHASE

year old children exhibit when gleefully running about the room nude after a bath.

Normally the first phase of early childhood sexual development, consisting of oral, aggressive and exhibitionistic-voyeuristic impulses, is passed through smoothly and usually gives only fleeting glimpses of its happening.

> "There is only one factor in childhood which has such central importance that its impairment calls for immediate action: that is the child's ability to develop, not to remain fixed to any (sexual) stage of development.
>
> "The seriousness of a childhood neurosis should be assessed not according to the damage which it does to the child but according to the degree in which it prevents the child from further (sexual) development."
>
> *The Psychoanalytical Treatment of Children*
> — by Anna Freud

Children **must not** be made to linger in these beginning stages of sexual growth. If misguided adults, sex educators or child molesters cause the child to linger in oral, aggressive or exhibitionistic-voyeuristic infantile sensual pleasures, an arrest, that is, a fixation in these early stages, may occur, and further forward sexual growth may cease. This is exactly what may result from sex programs given to 3 to 5 year old kindergarten students.

> "[Thirty] years ago, I and many other child analysts might have enthusiastically endorsed school sex education...because we believed at that time that emphasis on sexual knowledge could do no harm, only good. We have since learned that it is harmful to force sexual preoccupation on children... forcing of sexual preoccupation on the elementary school child is very likely to result in sexual difficulties in adulthood, and it can lead to disturbed behavior in childhood."
>
> — Rhoda L. Lorand, Ph.D.
> (Psychologist, New York City)

"...sensual impulses operate normally in the youngest children without any need for outside stimulation."

Freud's Letters 70 and 71 to W. Fliess

Kindergarten sex teachings consist of openly displaying nudity, of demonstrating male and female genital anatomy, and of showing how humans as well as some animals mate. The 3 to 5 year old has absolutely no need for such sex interferences. The instructions have no beneficial effect and can only serve to disrupt the child's further forward sexual growth by causing a fixation in early childhood sensual stages.

"Sexual interferences damage the child's forward movement of sexual development. Sex organization flows backward (regression) and attaches itself once more to earlier sensual wishes (fixation points). The ego of the child finds itself confronted with primitive desires (oral, aggressive, anal).

"From the developmental point of view, what counts is that sexual development is arrested in its course. Instead of moving on towards adult levels, it has been forced backwards, and important gains have thereby been undone. Qualities and achievements which depend directly on the stage of sexual growth are lost.

"The child who regresses to an oral level, for instance, reverts to emotional attitudes associated with it; it becomes more insatiable, impatient, "like a baby." Regression from the exhibitionistic-voyeuristic stage to the aggressive-anal stage destroys the hardly acquired attitudes of generosity, manliness and protectiveness and substitutes for them the domineering possessiveness which belongs to the earlier stage."

The Psychoanalytical Treatment of Children
— by Anna Freud

For example, repeated demonstrations of nudity and genital anatomy given in kindergarten sex classes cause undue intensification of and lingering in exhibitionism and voyeurism. As a result, forward sexual growth may cease, and "seeing and showing" become the main sexual aim from then on. In such cases, the eye replaces the genital organ as the primary sexual site in later life.

> "...there is no period at which the capacity for receiving and reproducing impressions is greater than precisely the years of childhood."
>
> — Sigmund Freud

> "Every environmental influence that hinders sexual growth will evidently lend support to the tendency to linger over the preparatory activities and turn them into new sexual aims that can take the place of the normal one."
>
> *Three Essays on the Theory of Sexuality*
> — by Sigmund Freud

Indeed, over the years, the widespread interferences by sex educators in the sexual development of the 3 to 5 year old can be seen in the ever increasing exhibitionism and voyeurism that has become part of our everyday culture. Pornographic books and magazines are available at practically every newsstand, and there are few, if any, movies that fail to show nudity and at least one intimate bedroom scene. Hundreds of millions of dollars are spent each year by today's young people just for pornographically-oriented videotapes and records alone. So it can be seen that what is learned in childhood leaves indelible impressions that remain throughout life.

The kindergarten sex instructions given to 3 to 5 year olds regarding mating causes still further problems. Psychoanalysis has shown that when a child is permitted to watch people mate (whether supervised by a sex teacher or not), the sex act is invariably regarded as a sadistic subjugation — that is, an abuse — of the female. The cruelty feelings in children subjected to such demonstrations of "coitus in the classroom" may be strengthened, and an excessive amount of sadism and masochism may come to play a major role in their adult sex life.

Another problem that may result from kindergarten sex education is that during the ages of 3 to 5 there are brief intervals in which the child has inclinations to fondle its genitals. If, through the teachings of sex instructors or a child molester, a child is encouraged to linger in such genital sex play and learns to obtain heightened satisfaction from the genital organ, the child is then usually obliged to repeat this satisfaction again and again. Through the instinct of repetition, incessant masturbation may continue right through childhood, into adolescence and adulthood. This would constitute a major deviation in normal, civilized sexual development. Consider for just one moment one example of what could happen as a result of such an aberration — a female child, for example, led to engage in repeated clitoral sex play by a child molester or kindergarten sex instructions, may grow up to become a nymphomaniac.

The life of a nymphomaniac is a shambles; for her, the sex act is merely a compulsive unaffectionate mechanical urge to repeat her early fixation in clitoral sex play. Any man who will participate with her is considered a suitable partner. Her appetite for sex is like the alcoholic's for liquor — she can never get enough, she is never satisfied, and she gets no pleasure from it. There is no worldly chance that she will ever be capable of making a mature, life sustaining sexual adjustment, irrespective of whether or not she gets married, has children or whatever.

"The sexual researches of these early years of childhood are always carried out in solitude. They constitute a first step towards taking an independent attitude in the world."

— Sigmund Freud

A brief review, then, of the harm done by kindergarten sex teachings given during the first phase of human sexual development is:

(1) Instructions given regarding nudity and genital anatomy may cause an arrest in forward sexual growth and produce a lifelong fixation in childhood exhibitionistic-voyeuristic sensual pleasures which become the primary sexual aim making a mature sexual adjustment in later life highly improbable.

(2) Demonstrations of mating given the 3 to 5 year old strengthen "aggressive-cruelty feelings" which may lead to sadistic-masochistic dispositions when these children grow up.

(3) Kindergarten sex teachings encourage an undue lingering in genital sex play which may cause continuous masturbation throughout childhood, adolescence and adulthood. Such masturbatory practices weaken character and preclude the development of mature adult sexuality.

Before concluding these brief comments on the first phase of sexual development and of the harm done by kindergarten sex programs, one important additional finding should be mentioned.

Contrary to the misinformation promulgated by sex educators that perversions, such as homosexuality, are due to "glandular or inherited conditions," over 100 years of psychoanalytic observations in real clinical settings have unequivocally shown that adult perverts are primarily a product of premature sexual experiences or seductions in early childhood.

This is true whether the seduction is due to actual attacks by a child molester, or whether the seduction is due to overexposures to sexual activities in sex classrooms or in the pornographic media.

"In the cases of many homosexuals, even 100% ones, it is possible to show that very early in their lives a sexual impression occurred which left a permanent after-effect in the shape of a tendency to homosexuality.

"In the case of many others, it is possible to point to environmental influences in their lives which have led sooner or later to a fixation of their homosexuality.

"Homosexuality can be removed by hypnotic suggestion, which would be astonishing in an inborn characteristic.

"...if the cases of allegedly inborn homosexuality were more closely examined, some experience of their early childhood would probably come to light which had a determining effect upon the direction taken by their sexuality. The experience would simply have passed out of the subject's conscious recollection, but could be recalled to his memory under appropriate influence."

Three Essays on the Theory of Sexuality
— by Sigmund Freud

SECOND PHASE

PHASE II

We now come to the second phase of human sexual development which occurs between the ages of 6 to 12.

As before, let us briefly look at the second phase of human sexual development, and at the same time consider the effects of today's public school sex education on 6 to 12 year old children.

The second sexual phase is referred to throughout the world as the "latency period." It is a period in which Nature causes direct sexual energies in the 6 to 12 year old to become dormant. There is nothing hypothetical about the latency period. It has been shown to exist throughout the world — in primitive as well as civilized people.

Vann Spruniell, M.D. (Psychoanalyst):

"They [psychiatrists] constantly observe latency — the real "McCoy", not just a deceptive appearance of it...during latency, the child develops an inner control system...

"During latency, adult communication with him about adult sex is an intrusion into an important and necessary privacy."

William McGrath, M.D. (Psychiatrist):

"There is a phase of personality development called the latency period, during which the healthy child is not interested in sex. This interval from about the age of five until adolescence serves a very important biological purpose. It affords a child an opportunity to develop his own resources, his beginning physical and mental strength.

"Premature interest in sex is unnatural and will arrest or distort the development of the personality. Sex education should not be foisted on children..."

Though direct sexual energies become quiescent during latency, these energies do not disappear, but are redirected by the 6 to 12 year old mind and are used to serve other purposes. For example, some redirected sexual energy is used for acquiring knowledge. This is why the 6 to 12 year old child is most educable.

"During the latency period, the child's interest in sexual matters largely subsides...

"Within the framework of the family, the child is now freed from the dross of sexuality. Tenderness takes the place of erotic needs, activity that of infantile aggression, etc."

from *"Prepuberty"*
— by Psychiatrist Helene Duetsch
Boston Psychoanalytic Institute

Prior to the establishment of today's public school sex teachings, teachers seemed to realize that involving the 6 to 12 year old child in sexual matters made the child ineducable, and they made every effort to avoid arousing the child sexually.

"In so far as educators pay any attention to childhood sexuality...they behave as though they knew that sexual activity makes a child ineducable."

— Sigmund Freud

Repeated scholastic tests done on today's sexually educated 6 to 12 year old children indeed show that these students have accomplished less scholastically than pre-sex education students.

"Sociologists Peter R. Uhlenberg and David Eggebeen of the University of North Carolina focus on the changes in the welfare of white teenagers from 1960 to 1980, as indicated by statistics measuring their educational performance, moral character, and physical health.

"The facts are not very reassuring. In the 20-year interval, the Scholastic Aptitude Test scores of college-bound high school seniors declined steeply, and the delinquency rates, drug use, and childbirth and abortion rates for unmarried teenage women all rose sharply.

"Whatever the reasons for these disturbing trends, economic factors do not appear to be primary ones. The authors point out that the incidence of poverty among white youths 16 and 17 years old, for example, declined by 60% from 1960 to 1980. In the same period, real per-pupil expenditures in U.S. public schools doubled, a change reflected in both a drop in class size and an increase in the percentage of teachers with graduate degrees. Federal social programs aimed at the young also proliferated.

"In short, write Uhlenberg and Eggebeen, 'spending more money to improve the environments of children has not brought about an improvement in their well-being.' "

from *Economic Diary*

The educability of children is not all that is at stake when latency is disturbed by classroom sex interferences. For example, during latency, some redirected sexual energy is used for development of compassion. Compassion is essential for the control of cruelty impulses in the human. Compassion is one of the elements that truly separates man from all other creatures. If compassion fails to develop during latency due to direct sexual energies being kept stirred up by school sex teachings, it is most unlikely to develop at any other time in life. Persons whose compassionate feelings are destroyed during latency by sex education are frequently devoid of this emotion.

"The absence of the barrier of compassion brings with it the danger that the connection between cruelty and the sexual instincts may prove unbreakable."

— Sigmund Freud

In addition to these things already mentioned, latency makes invaluable contributions to personal and cultural achievements. And finally, and most important, latency is also responsible for strengthening inborn mental barriers that control base sexual and aggressive instincts. These mental barriers or "restraints" consist of feelings of shame, disgust, moral ideas, aesthetics, pain, horror, etc. These barriers are inborn and are essential for controlling raw sexual, aggressive and brutal instincts.

To be effective in later life, inborn mental barriers must be strengthened during the years of 6 to 12 by family, school and religion.

Instead of strengthening these controls, however, school sex courses use every educational technique known to break down these natural mental barriers. Removing mental controls over base sexuality is completely contrary to and destructive to family life and normal civilized sexuality.

> "Our civilization is founded on the suppression of instincts. Each individual has contributed some renunciation...
>
> "Over and above the struggle for existence, it is chiefly family feeling... which has induced the individuals to make this renunciation. This renunciation... is sanctioned by religion."
>
> *Sexuality and the Psychology of Love*
> — by Sigmund Freud

Not infrequently, sex educators applaud the unrestrained, brazen attitudes of their sexually instructed 6 to 12 year old students, and proclaim that such personality traits are evidence of increased self-confidence. However, the personality traits that the educators applaud are usually the early characteristics of an uncaring psychopath — that is, an individual who has no concern for anyone but himself or others in so far as they can serve some purpose for him.

The psychopathy in today's sexually educated 6 to 12 year old children has reached alarming proportions. Preteen murders, pregnancies, prostitution, criminality and venereal diseases are no

THIRD
PHASE

longer uncommon. This increase in crimes, violence and sex over the past twenty years is even more shocking when one considers that the 6 to 12 year old child, who has not been sexually disturbed, is normally a most responsible individual and one least likely to be involved in sociopathic behavior.

> "Among the instincts, the sexual instincts are conspicuous for their strength and savagery. Woe, if they should be set loose!"
>
> from *Character and Culture*
> — by Sigmund Freud

To sum-up, then — some adverse effects of the sex education courses given to 6 to 12 year old children are:

(1) Sex teachings make the 6 to 12 year old student less educable;

(2) The courses can block the development of compassionate feelings;

(3) The sex indoctrinations weaken mental barriers controlling base sexuality and brutality, thereby making the child vulnerable to perversions and violence; and

(4) The teachings hamper social, cultural and personal achievements.

PHASE III

We now come to the third phase of human sexual development and to the sex courses given to adolescent students. The third phase begins in puberty, around the age of thirteen, and continues throughout adolescence into early adulthood. In this final phase of sexual development, latency comes to an end, and direct sexual feelings are once again reawakened. In the case of 13-14 year old boys, the reawakened sexual energies are straightforward and are centered in the male genitalia. The reawakened erotic feelings of pubescent girls follow a **much** different course.

FANTASY

Because a girl's genital structures are (1) biologically unready, and (2) remain vaginally anesthetic to sexual intercourse until much later in life, and (3) because her feminine psychology is not completed until late adolescence, nature has provided the young female with a "natural aversion" to sexual intercourse.

Though nature has provided the teenage girl with a natural aversion to engaging in the vaginal sex act, her sensual feelings may be as intense as the boy's. Her desires, however, are not for genital intercourse, but, instead, involve sexual fantasies and dreams, kisses and caresses, the wish to love and be loved, tender words of love, and sometimes thoughts of having a child. Her eroticisms, however, are not inseparably entwined with the sex act such as they are in the male.

Sensual love fantasies in adolescence are natural, beneficial, and gratifying. However, they are not meant to be carried out in real life.

Adolescent sexual fantasies are essential for normal sexual development in both sexes. Unfortunately, classroom sex teachings suppress fantasy life by openly, or tacitly encouraging direct sexual activities. For example, some school sex instructors place condoms in Valentine greeting cards and send these cards to students with the wish for a "Happy Valentines Day". The only admonition given by these sex teachers is that before engaging in sex, students should use multi-colored, multi-flavored condoms freely available at school based health [sex] clinics.

Today's sexually educated teenage female, who fails to abide by her natural feminine inhibitions, and is led by sex teachings and peer pressures to prematurely engage in sex, reacts with feelings of disappointment, coldness and emptiness. Due to engaging in intercourse prematurely, her feminine psychology fails to develop, her feminine emotions become dry and sterile and a life-long conflict develops between herself and her inner femininity and motherhood feelings. [The makings for tody's extreme feminine activist.]

The dichotomy between the adolescent boy's readiness for sex and the girl's natural sexual inhibition serves a vital purpose. Nature always has a reason for what it does. The girl's reluctance to

the sex act serves to strengthen the affectionate and spiritual nature of sex.

Adolescent chastity in boys and girls is essential for development of affectionate feelings and for the spiritualization of sex. Through sexual spiritualization, adolescents learn to regard sex and the sex partner with utmost importance. Through sexual spiritualization, youths learn to feel esteem for members of the opposite sex. In the male, this esteem is especially felt for girls who are chaste — and is usually lacking for girls who are easily had.

Sexual spiritualization leads to the idealization of a "special someone" of the opposite sex which makes life complete for both partners. The answer is *not* that 1 + 1 = 2, but that a half + half makes one whole person. This is the foundation for monogamous love upon which civilized families are built in a democratic society.

When affectionate needs are not met during sexual intercourse and physical sex is all that remains, frustrations develop which frequently lead to serious depressions. For relief from these mental depressions, many of today's sexually active youths turns to perversions, alcohol, drugs, and, not infrequently, suicide. Adolescents admitted to hospitals for depressions have tripled, and suicide has increased by 200% since the establishment of school sex education. An epidemic of adolescent suicides is sweeping the United States. Teenage suicides now rank as the first leading cause of death in young people under 21 [including deaths from accidents due to drunk driving], and the incidence of suicide in unmarried teenage girls is several times higher than the national average.

In the March 21, 1985 edition of the *Los Angeles Jewish Community Bulletin*, psychiatrist, Dr. Richard Bloom, reports that the dramatic rise in teen suicides can be directly attributed to the sex life of today's young adolescent. Psychiatrist Bloom says, "Having extremely active sex lives by the time they're 14, teenagers have lost that feeling of looking forward to a special someone. Most kids have been through every kind of sexual experience by the time they're 16."

**1972-1988
Here Lies Our Betsy**

"Many acts of gangsterism, prostitution or criminality in young girls are the consequence of a violent interruption of early puberty with its harmless girl-girl relationships by heterosexual acts for which they are not yet really ready...

"Premature heterosexual experiences produce disturbances in the development of a girl's whole personality."

from *The Psychology of Women*
— by Helene Deutsch, M.D.

C. VALUES AND STANDARDS

Let's digress for a moment and take a look at the morality, values and standards that Planned Parenthood type school sex programs give junior and senior high school students. The values and standards taught go out of their way to depreciate the values and morals of parents and the Judeo-Christian religions.

"The conscience of an adult is the representative of moral demands made by the society in which he/she lives. We know it owes its origin to the identification with the parents. To the parents society has transferred the task of establishing ethical aims on the child and enforcing the restrictions upon instincts.

"If parents are depreciated by the environment in the pre-adolescent or adolescent eyes, the youth's conscience already constructed by the parents is in danger of being lost or depreciated too, so that it cannot oppose instinctual impulses which press for satisfaction. The origin of many anti-social and character abnormalities can be explained in this way."

from *The Psychoanalytic Treatment of Children*
— Anna Freud

The consciences instilled in the minds of children by parents are decimated by the school sex programs. Under the leadership of

sex
education

teacher's
guide
and
resource
manual

planned
parenthood
santa cruz
county

sex teachers, inexperienced youths are taught to set up their own values that, in fact, consist of having no values at all. Students are led to believe that values simply depend upon "enjoying what you do and do what you enjoy."

Despite recent studies done by an international educational testing service that reports..."American teenagers come out at the bottom of the heap...scholastically...and reveal a weakness in higher order thinking skills," students in sex classes are advised to put aside the teachings of parents and 5,000 years of human history and to determine for themselves what is correct sexual behavior, and to make their own decisions as to whether or not to engage in sex. To help students make these vital decisions, they are led to rely on the "sex is for fun" transgressions of *Planned Parenthood - SIECUS* organizations and the sexual propaganda of homosexual activists.

Should these statements about the values and standards promoted by sex educators seem exaggerated, an examination of any ordinary "sex education teacher's guide and resource manual" should be made — as for example, the manuals sponsored throughout the United States by Planned Parenthood and its related organizations. In the Planned Parenthood teachers' "Guide and Resource Manual" used in Santa Cruz, California* (which is typical of guides and manuals used throughout the United States), the "Sexuality and Values Section" consists entirely of three topics only:

(1) The first of these three topics is "Human Sexual Responses" based on the reports of 300 or so paid and unpaid volunteers and prostitutes used by Masters and Johnson to engage in sex acts while monitored by viewers and electronic devices.

(2) The second topic discussed in the "Sexuality and Values" section is masturbation. The masturbation discussion consists of explaining and sanctioning all forms of masturbation that lead to orgasmic emissions. If parents object of open masturbation, students are told to masturbate more privately in order to avoid family arguments.

*Available by sending $20.00 to Planned Parenthood, 212 Laurel Street, Santa Cruz, CA 95060.

Illustration from
Killers of Children

(3) The final topic discussed in the "Sexuality and Values" section — a section that is supposed to somehow be teaching values and standards — is homosexuality. Homosexuality is taught as a normal variation, i.e., a normal lifestyle. The manuals advise sex teachers to bring homosexuals directly into the classroom to give students first-hand information about how homosexuals conduct themselves sexually. Students are taught that the homosexual's oral-genital sex acts, his oral-anal acts, his self and mutual masturbation, etc. are normal and beneficial. The only prerequisite for engaging in homosexual-lesbian sex acts, students are taught, is that one enjoy them.

Sodomy is regarded as normal sexual practice that is equivalent to heterosexual genital intercourse. Because of recent intensified demands from pro-homosexuals and homosexual activists, homosexuality and lesbianism are glorified in school classrooms more than ever.

The sexual values and standards taught in Planned Parenthood sponsored sex programs have nothing to do with sexual morality. The teachings are simply condonations of indifferent sex acts with indifferent sex partners, glorifications of perverts, approbation of masturbation and instructions in contraception and abortion.

> "FACT: 'Planned Parenthood's youth activities amount, in effect, to a positive encouragement of sexual activity among teenagers. Showering these young people with contraceptives and provocative literature results in a tremendous peer pressure that makes teenagers who do not engage in sex feel abnormal.
>
> *Facts About Planned Parenthood*
> — by Paul Marx. Ph.D. and Judie Brown

Despite teachers satisfying some state laws by going through the formality of advising students to remain chaste until marriage, nevertheless, there is one main overriding theme in today's school sex programs — and that theme is *carnality*. School sex teachings are essentially "how to" courses that condone and teach fornication along with all forms of perversion.

Some teachers, for example, a sex teacher at Long Beach California State College, awarded extra credits to students who participated in perversions [physically and psychologically destructive sexual activities] and reported their perverted experiences openly in the classroom. Such horrendous teachings not only create perverts out of some students, but an over-tolerance for perverts is instilled in the minds of all students. This undue over-tolerance — promoted as "understanding others" — destroys the natural mental defense mechanism to shun the pervert as a means of avoiding contamination. As a result students are left defenseless.

> "Among contributory forces working against perversions... authoritative prohibition by society is a chief factor. Where homosexuality is not regarded as a crime it will be found in no small number of people."
>
> *Transformation of Puberty*
> — by Sigmund Freud

Teaching youths an over-tolerance for perverts and an acceptance of the belief that orgasm achieved by any means is beneficial, can lead young people into becoming soulless, polymorphous, "mechanical robots" capable of engaging in any kind of sex act with indifference and without guilt. *These are the characteristics of prostitutes and pimps.*

The goal of a boy should be to become a man, and that of a girl to become a woman. The development of femininity and the feminine woman (humankind's greatest gift) require an undisturbed adolescent sexual maturation.

Along with carnal teachings, all sex courses provide detailed information on contraception and abortion. It seems ludicrous, but after desensitizing the minds of students year after year to carnality, sex educators have the temerity to claim that their courses can prevent teen and preteen pregnancies if only the public would be even more supportive of school sex programs and school-based "health clinics."

Ed. Update: Is that how the [health] clinics are advertised?

Brown: They are never advertised initially as having anything whatsoever to do with sexuality. They are promoted within communities as filling a need for total health and welfare services. It is said that these clinics will provide free physicals, and that children who are suffering from aches and pains of whatever nature will be able to come to the clinic for reliable on-campus medical services. The main argument against that, of course, is if that were truly the only purpose for the existence of a school-based health clinic, then what has the nurse been doing?

Ed. Update: What is the philosophy of health clinic proponents? What do they really want?

Brown: The goal of those who promote these clinics is to encourage children to be very mechanical about their sexuality. Rather than cherish our human sexuality as a gift, as something very unique about each and every one of us, children are encouraged to behave like animals. Setting aside all moral convictions, there is no provider of birth control for children today who warns them of the threat of pelvic inflammatory disease for the young girl who goes on the pill or the threat of AIDS for anybody who fools around outside of marriage.

It is very interesting to debate Dr. Laurie Zabin, author of the study of a Baltimore clinic, because she refuses to discuss the health aspects of the pill, or of promiscuity as it relates to venereal disease. She can only tout the two findings of her study. The first is that by having a sex clinic in the school the average teenager, according to anonymous questionnaires, delayed her first intercourse for seven months. The 13-year old, in other words, waited until she was almost 14 or the 15-year old waited until she was almost 16. that is a victory according to Dr. Zabin.

The other touted success is that the pregnancy rate decreased. The only reason the pregnancy rate decreased in the Baltimore study, the St. Paul Clinic study, or the Chicago Du Sable High School study is that they never counted abortions. In Maryland, for example, one-third of the abortions are performed on adolescent children, and yet the Baltimore study never mentions the word abortion because they do not figure terminated pregnancies in the pregnancy count.

Ed. Update: Has the incidence of abortion risen in the past few years?

Brown: The teenage abortion rate has quadrupled since the inception of birth control information in the classroom (1970). We do not know how much higher the abortion rate will go with the existence of sex clinics in a given school because those who administer sex clinic programs always ignore abortion.

from *The American Heritage Foundation:*
"Education Update," 1986

Curbing Births, Not Pregnancies
by Stan E. Weed

More than a million teenagers — most of them unmarried —
become pregnant each year, and the number is rising. The belief is
widespread that the number will be reduced by opening more
"family-planning" clinics and making them more accessible to
teens. However, research a colleague and I have done suggests
otherwise.

As the number and proportion of teenage family-planning
clinics increased, we observed a corresponding increase in the teenage pregnancy and abortion rates: 50 to 120 more teenage pregnancy per 1,000 clients, rather than the 200 to 300 fewer pregnancies as
estimated by researchers at the Alan Guttmacher Institute (former-
ly the research arm of the Planned Parenthood Federation). We did
find that greater teenage participation in such clinics led to lower
teen birthrates. However, the impact on the abortion and total pregnancy rates was exactly opposite the stated intentions of the program. The original problems appear to have grown worse.

Our research has been under way for two years, and analyzes
data from such reliable sources as the Centers for Disease Control,
the Guttmacher Institute, and U.S. Census data for all 50 states
and the District of Columbia. Since pregnancy, abortion and
birthrates also vary with such factors as urbanization, mobility,
race and poverty, these variables were also taken into account for
each state. Our findings have twice sustained formal review by
specialists in the field.

(Mr. Weed is director of the independent Institute for Research
and Evaluation in Salt Lake City. His two studies with Joseph A.
Olsen cited here were published recently in the journal *Family
Perspective.*)

The Wall Street Journal
Tuesday, October 14, 1986

"As one student said, 'If the clinic is going to give [condoms] to you, it's telling you, 'Go ahead. Have sex.' Since they're giving it out, why not?'

"The reduction in teen-pregnancy rates that is claimed as a result of the SBC's has been achieved by an increase in teen abortion, not by a reduction in teen sex activity."

— Charles E. Rice, Professor of Law, Notre Dame University

The callous persuasiveness used to teach students about abortions has so desensitized students to abortion that should a sexually educated girl become pregnant, she submits to having these psychologically mutilating operations with about as much concern as having a manicure. Indeed, to meet the demands of today's unwed teen pregnancies, abortion clinics have become as commonplace as beauty parlors.

"Olga has an abortion to separate himself from her child in order to be free to work for the 'cause'.

"Genia undergoes an abortion without displaying the slightest sign of the normal feminine reaction to this experience. She has no time to give birth to a child or to love it.

"So this is how the attitudes have been transformed in the past [thirty years!] Is this progress, and does this progress bring more freedom and potentialities of happiness to women — or is such freedom won at the price of inability to experience the most intense feminine happiness?"

from *Psychology of Women*
— by Helen Deutsch, M.D.

When schools go out of their way to teach the mechanics of fornication and sex acts associated with perversions, students get the impression they are being told: "Go ahead and do it." Today's sexually educated, sexually active youths do not represent a new breed of emancipated youths who under the guiding patronage of a progressive educational system have developed keen insights

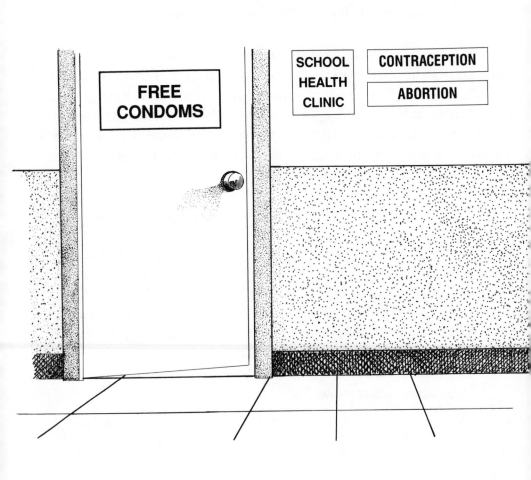

into human sexuality. They are simply misled young people who have been rushed into "sham-sex" by benighted sex educators.

Despite arguments to the contrary given by Planned Parenthood and sex educators, the fact is that there has been an ever increasing number of unwed preteen and teen pregnancies since public school sex programs and "school based health clinics" have come into existence. Millions of teenagers become pregnant each year. In 1979, for example, it was determined that 5,000,000 adolescent girls between the ages of 15 and 19 engaged in sexual intercourse. One year later, in 1980, 1,100,000 pregnancies occurred in these 5,000,000 sexually active 15 to 19 year old girls. This statistical information does not begin to include the number of pregnancies in the **10 to 14 year old sexually educated girls**.

Such statistics were unprecedented prior to today's sex education. Dr. C. A. Domz, in his article appearing in the *Medical Economics Magazine,* had it right when he said that one would require 20-20 ostrich vision to dismiss such statistics as coincidence.

The truth is — "There are none so blind as those who will not see."

The Allan Guttmacher Institute, a former major activistic arm of Planned Parenthood, openly places the blame for today's preteen and teen pregnancies on American manufacturers for not developing better contraceptives for sexually educated students. The Guttmacher Institute and Planned Parenthood sex educators do not begin to place the blame on themselves for the sexual disasters in many of today's young people, but they point their fingers accusingly at parents and the U.S. Congress for not providing even more funds for their school sex programs. The fact is that the U.S. Planned Parenthood organization is so highly funded by American taxpayers that it is now aggressively attempting to spend some of their excess monies for promoting school sex programs and contraception-abortion "school based health sex clinics" into schools of other nations.

Illustration from
Killers of Children

**SEX EDUCATION
PROPONENTS**

PARENTS

CONGRESS

Illustration from
Killers of Children

"I have never seen a greater interest in money... They are very good at getting their funds from a Congress seemingly enraptured by the pieties, pontifications, and poor-mouthings of higher education. But very few words can be heard from any of these representatives about...purpose, quality, curriculum, the moral authority and responsibilities of universities."

— Former Secretary of the Department of
Education William Bennett

FACT: Planned Parenthood receives charitable contributions from many chapters of the United Way and similar groups. In 1980 the organization's budget was about $140.8 million, at least $69.7 million of which was paid by the American Taxpayers.

Facts About Planned Parenthood
— by Paul Marx, Ph.D and Judie Brown

Numerous repeated scientific studies clearly show that as school sex education programs increase, unwed pregnancies, abortions, perversions, prostitution, and suicides increase proportionally.

NEW STUDY: GOVERNMENT-FUNDED BIRTH CONTROL, SEX ED LEAD TO INCREASE IN TEENAGE PREGNANCIES

Providing taxpayer funded contraceptives and abortions to teenagers is leading to an increase, rather than a decrease, in teen pregnancies. So concludes a recently-released study by Professor Jacqueline Kasun, Ph.D., of Humboldt State University.

According to Dr. Kasun's spring 1986 report, entitled "Teenage Pregnancy: What Comparisons Among States and Countries Show," "comparisons among states and countries provide no support of the claim that government birth control can reduce pregnancy,... considerable evidence that restrictions on access, especially in the form of requirements for parental consent, can reduce pregnancy."

Dr. Kasun's research reveals that there are large variations in teenage pregnancy rates and programs among the American states. What is interesting, the research said, is a state-by-state comparison of those statistics.

Dr. Kasun found that four states led the rest in 1980 for (1) providing free access to publicly-funded abortion and (2) having spent higher than the national average amounts per person on publicly-funded birth control. Those states are California, Hawaii, Georgia, and New York.

Those states do not require parental consent or notification for minors' contraceptives or abortions, and abortions are provided at public expense.

Rather than experiencing a reduction in the number of teen pregnancies and abortions, Dr. Kasun's research discovered that "all four states have higher-than-average teenage pregnancy rates as well as higher-than-average of teenage abortion-plus-unmarried births."

Statistical testing by the method of rank correlation showed that "states that spend relatively large amounts on government birth control also tend to have high rates of teenage abortion-plus-unmarried births." Those states include Georgia, Vermont, South Carolina, and Tennessee.

But those states which spent the least on birth control and abortion tended to have the lowest rates of abortions-plus-unmarried births. Those states include Utah, South Dakota, Idaho, and North Dakota.

Programs Create Problems

"It may be argued that state programs for the control of teenage pregnancy are responses to problems, not causes of them," states Kasun. "The facts, however, suggest that the programs create problems." The researcher uses the California experience as her case in point.

California has consistently spent more than twice as much as the national average on government birth control, cites Kasun. In FY 1971-73, the California State Office of Family Planning spent $4 million. But by 1983, spending had increased to where the state spent $95 million a year on contraceptives, sterilizations, and abortions.

During this period, "the teenage pregnancy rate in California rose to a level that was 30% above the national level, and the teenage abortion rate more than tripled, to a level that was 60% above the national level."

In 1981, almost 60% of teenage pregnancies in California were aborted, compared with 45% for the nation.

According to Dr. Kasun, California promoted and provided sex education at all grade levels during this period, sent pregnancy counselors into schools, and promoted contraceptives and abortions to teenagers at public expense without notifying parents.

Reduced access means reduced pregnancies

Based on statistical evidence, Dr. Kasun also suggests that "there is additional evidence... that unwanted teenage pregnancy may be reduced not by increasing teenagers' access to birth control but by restricting it."

To support her claim, Dr. Kasun points out that "during the 1970's, the state of South Dakota reduced its use of Title X family planning funds, and there occurred a reduction in teenage pregnancy."

Similarly, "in 1980 the state of Utah passed a law requiring parental consent for minors to be given birth control, and rates of pregnancy and abortion among girls 15-17 fell."

In 1981, the state of Minnesota passed a law requiring parents to be notified of minors' abortions.

"There ensued dramatic reductions in abortions, births, and pregnancies," states Kasun. "The teenage abortion rate fell by 20% between 1980 and 1983, the pregnancy rate by 16%, and the fertility rate by 13%."

And, "in 1984, an English court prohibited giving prescription contraceptives to girls under 16; there ensued a decrease in abortions among this age group."

Nowhere do the sex educators make the slightest suggestion that their devastating sex programs rank among the greatest tragedies that our nation has ever endured and that their sex courses should be stopped. Nowhere do they explain why schools have summarily assumed the right to inculcate carnality into the minds of students while at the same time they disclaim any responsibility for upholding sexual morality. Nor do they explain who gave teachers the authority to act as sexual counselors and to dismantle the parents' responsibilities for their children's natural development. At no time do the sex teachers remotely suggest that the *cure* for today's (1) teen pregnancies, (2) prostitution, (3) venereal diseases, (4) criminality and (5) suicides necessitates that the educational system upholds the family and respects basic Judeo-Christian morality — a morality that supports the struggle for existence, sustains civilized life and a morality that is in line with the world's enduring religions — *and a morality, whose life sustaining nature is unequivocally substantiated by psychoanalytic observations.*

"Physicians are treating more and more sick girls... performing more abortions and coping with a pandemic of venereal disease... From a medical standpoint, there is much to wonder about a [sexual] revolution that precipitates so much physical and mental suffering."

C.A. Domz, M.D., "Doctors Against Pornography"
Medical Economics Magazine.

"Teachers from many parts of North America...declared that it seemed to them hardly worthwhile to try to teach high school youngsters about venereal diseases because they seemed so indifferent and defiant... Venereal diseases represent a challenge not merely to medical science but to morality — if one dare use such an old-fashioned word."

Paul Popenoe, ScD, (Director of The American Institute of Family Relations), in an article, "A Contribution To The Dialogue On Sex Education"
Child and Family Magazine.

Sexually Transmissible Organisms in Adolescent Girls

"A sexually active 15-year-old girl is estimated to have a one in eight chance of acquiring acute pelvic inflammatory disease...

"The overall prevalence of six sexually transmittible organisms as related to sexual activity status...were all isolated significantly more frequently from sexually active girls than from virginal girls. **Neisseria gonorrhoea** and **Trichomonas vaginalis** were isolated exclusively from sexually active girls."

from *Pediatrics*, April 1986
vol. 77, p. 488

The sex educators have either a mental block — that is a strong repression — or, for some reason, cannot see that their sex programs are largely responsible for the wanton sexual behavior so prevalent in many young people.

The sex educators not only deny their accountability, but some rashly blame parents, rather than themselves, for the pregnancies, gutter sex and venereal diseases that are rife among many young people today. Indeed, many sex educators portray themselves as saviors of youths by professing to protect students from the outmoded established standards and values of parents whose sexualities, the sex educators say, have been stunted by anachronistic morals and religion. The teachers object to parents expecting schools and colleges to teach or uphold sexual decency and sexual morality. These topics, the educators proclaim, are "religious" and illegal for schools.

"During the past 14 years, Planned Parenthood and its allies have hoodwinked legislators and bureaucrats into thinking that parental involvement will only exacerbate teen pregnancy rather than relieve it. Something as serious as this, so they say, should be left to the doctor and patient exclusively. Parents need not apply.

"Time and events have proven them wrong. In Minnesota, where a 1981 law required parental notification for abortion, the pregnancy, abortion and birth rates among adolescents plummeted. According to a 1985 report by the House Select Committee on Children, Youth and Families, from 1980 to 1983, abortions to Minnesota teens, 15-19, dropped 40 percent; the teen birth rate decreased 23.4 percent and pregnancies decreased 32 percent. In the same period, the number of teens, 15-19, decreased by only 13.5 percent.

"A similar trend in England was reported following a 1984 court case making it illegal for doctors to prescribe contraceptives to minors without parental consent."

"Focus: Contraceptives for Children, a Parental Control Battle"
— by Senator Jesse Helms

All too frequently, some parents are persuaded to relinquish their own sensibilities in deference to the sex teachers. Such parents are led to believe that "teacher knows best," and many of these mothers and fathers become zealous advocates for public school sex programs.

TIDBITS...

"Up to 600,000 children under the age of 16 are engaged in prostitution. Between 300,000 and 600,000 children younger than 16 years old are used in child pornography, appearing in more than 264 publications."

from *CDL Reporter*

Recently (1988) a Chicago newspaper casually reported that 80% of the freshman to senior female enrollment in a Chicago high school were pregnant.

PARENTS

WE SUPPORT
MRS. JONES
SEX EDUCATION
CLASS.

REMEMBER...
TEACHERS
KNOW BEST!

The national sexual calamity among many of our youths remains unabated. The question is — have the teachings of the sex educators and the influence of the pornographic entertainment media so thoroughly persuaded the public to accept preteen/teen sex, free love and perversions that they have already brought our nation to the "point of no return?"

"A new very explicit 'soap opera' is playing on cable TV in major cities across the U.S. It is entitled 'Forbidden Promises' and is...a very candid and explicit look at the homosexual lifestyle as perceived by the producers — showing this lifestyle in a positive light.

"...It is actually showing men kissing and in bed together, all on TV coming right into our own living rooms...

"...[it] is promoted as a positive lifestyle and is...crammed down the throats of...Americans who support traditional family values."

Newsletter: Concerned Women of America

Dr. Lawrence J. Hatterer of Cornell University, in a paper given before the American Academy of Psychoanalysis, concluded that homosexuality could be triggered by environmental stimuli. Among the most important triggers, Dr. Hatterer said, are homosexual literature, plays and movies.

The National Institute of Mental Health, in a newly published report based on a review of 2,500 research studies, reported:

"After a decade of gathering evidence, the consensus among most of the research community is that violence on television does lead to aggressive behavior by children and teenagers who watch the programs.

"There is an average of five violent acts per hour on prime time and eighteen acts per hour on children's weekend programs.

"Entertainment television has become an important sex educator. Extramarital affairs are shown on TV five times as often as sexual activities by married couples." [Would it be anymore efficacious if sexual activities of only married couples were shown? Incidentally, no mention is made of the perverted sex shown on TV.]

DAILY TIMES

MOVIES

THE PERFECT WEAPON
GUILTY BY SUSPICION
SLEEPING WITH THE ENEMY
THE SILENCE OF THE LAMBS
IF LOOKS COULD KILL
PREDATOR

D. WHAT CAN BE DONE?

Assuming that the point of no return has not been reached, what can be done?

FIRST, I believe the sexually gangrenous material filling the minds of young people as a result of today's sex education and the pornographic entertainment media must stop forming. A tourniquet preventing further spread of contamination is urgently needed.

Planned Parenthood type sex educators must be led to know that we have had enough.

Local, state and national school officials must be led to know that we expect them to translate our outrage into educational courses that serve the needs of civilized people!...not the needs of unrestrained barbarians.

There can be no compromise — free love and perversions promoted by school sex programs cannot exist side by side with mature love and family life. Each destroys the other.

SECONDLY, to stop the decline of Western Civilization by the vilification of human sexuality, a social conscience must be reestablished in our nation...a conscience that will not abide non-life-sustaining gutter sex to be spewed out publicly, a social conscience that will not sanction pornography because a court decides such sexual evil is *lawful* if it meets "community standards" or contains a figment of some "socially redeeming something," and a conscience that will not tolerate sexual indecency becoming a cultural norm by corrupt interpretations of the 1st Amendment of the Constitution.

Is such a conscience censorious? Of course. It is the purpose of a conscience to control coarse, base, raw instincts which comprises all that is evil in mankind. Anyone who contends that consciences should not control one's "individual freedom" because it violates the 1st Amendment corrupts this important national law and advocates that our society revert to mankind's primordial beginnings-a time when there were no restraints.

Illustration from
Killers of Children

A complete absence of traditional government and unrestrained lawlessness seems the ultimate goals of those determined to give free expressions to all manners of human behavior by invoking the 1st Amendment.

Perhaps 2,000 or so years hence mankind may develop individual consciences that will sufficiently control ancestrally inherited instincts making an overall social conscience unnecessary. But in the meantime life-sustaining controls remain essential.

In conclusion, two matters stand out:

— The first is that for the continued existence of **life sustaining sex** which completely depends upon "affectionate, monogamous, man/woman, long lasting love relationship," it is as necessary to eradicate today's *"psychological sexual diseases"* as it is to eradicate today's physical sexual diseases such as AIDS.

— And secondly for the survival of a civilization based on families composed of individuals living by consciences instead of barbarians living by instincts only, it is essential that sexual decency be maintained, not only in our homes, but also in the schools to which we send our children.

> "In our social structure built up over hundreds of years, the family constitutes the individual's first environment...
>
> "Cultural factors can, nevertheless, be so powerful that they extensively modify human behavior."
>
> *Psychology of Women*
> — Helene Deutsch, M.D.

...AND RELATED MATTERS

CHAPTER ONE

CHASTITY, ABSTINENCE, AND VIRGINITY

After working long and hard to eradicate "Planned Parenthood type" sex programs,years of incessant conditioning have persuaded many such parents that "some sort of school sex education is absolutely necessary." Planned Parenthood has spooked and spoofed these people into believing school sex teachings are a necessary part of school curriculums-if for no other reason than their adult sons and daughters will be unable to obey inherited sexual impulses, and humankind will become an endangered species.

The relatively recent development of "Chastity and Abstinence" programs is regarded by some as a solution to the problem: of providing "some kind of sex program."

At first, a sex course with a very alluring title *Sex Respect* was one of the first programs thought to be the answer. "Sex Respect" was what parents were wanting for their children. This course, developed by Coleen Mast, a former *Planned Parenthood* sex teacher, I find, is simply a mitigated mirror image of Planned Parenthood sex programs. Many proponents of "some kind of sex education" are indeed becoming leery of the Mast *Sex Respect* course. 　　　　　　　　　　　　　　　　　 * Oriented

More recently, some new "Chastity and Abstinence" programs have become enthusiastically received. The main purpose of these "C and A" programs is to salvage some students who have been ravaged by years of K-12 sex school indoctrination.

"C and A" teachers largely comprise a cadre of young adult females-and some males- who have managed to maintain their chastity or who have themselves suffered sexual catastrophes related to Planned Parenthood type sex teachings. These young people act as teacher/therapists and are devoted to helping other sexually educated abused students.

Unmarried pregnant, sexually promiscuous, or sexually depressed students are warmly and solicitously counseled by the new "C & A" teachers. The counseling consists primarily of desensitizing students to the pernicious belief that sexual activity is normal and necessary in order to be accepted by the teenage society. "C & A" teachers attempt to convince sexually educated youths — many of whom are no longer virginal — that sex is *not* engaged in by ALL their peers. Young people counseled by the "C & A" teachers seem astonished to learn that many teenagers "just say 'no!'" The "C & A" teachers encourage these confused youths to join "just say 'no' chastity and abstinence groups" where they are readily accepted, not rejected.

"C & A" programs do not include the word "virginity" because, perhaps, the teachers realize the word would make "C & A" courses seem too puritanical or "old- fashioned" for modern youths. (In many schools today, 13 year old girls are ritualistically expected to lose their virginity by the time they become 14. The boy or man whom the girl chooses to "deflower" her is totally unimportant.)

"C & A" teachers provide an invaluable service in helping sexually defiled adolescent girls (and boys) restore their lives. These teachers should be commended.

Unfortunately, "C & A" programs are no match for the highly funded Planned Parenthood Organization, who in recent years has convinced many parents "not to be 'hypocritical' and to openly admit that their sons and daughters copulate freely." Parents are further admonished to accompany their children to school contraceptive [health] clinics or else accept responsibility for the in-

crease of unwed pregnancies and abortions in their daughters.

Unfortunately, "C & A" courses are analogous to "closing the barn door after the horse has gotten out." The courses succor and reassure children and youths disturbed by Planned Parenthood's sex teachings, but fail to protect them before established Planned Parenthood courses have had their effects.

For some students, the "C & A" counseling works. However, "C & A" courses would be unnecessary if school sex teachings were not a part of todays school curricula.

"C & A" programs are only weak antidotes for the ruinous effects of K-12 sex education. But who would not agree that any help is better than nothing. The most effective "C & A" programs are conducted by students themselves. In any event, "C & A" programs, unfortunately, are not the solution to the countless sexual problems resulting from today's school sex education.

The solution is... STOP SIECUS-PLANNED PARENTHOOD'S SCHOOL SEX PROGRAMS. To accomplish this, all that is needed is for our nation to simply not permit sex educators, social reformers and sexperts to use school children as guinea pigs for testing out sexual folderol.

Parents should open their minds to what schools are truly doing to their children. A stout punch should be given to temeritous teachers who threaten: "If parents don't teach their children all about sex, then we will do the job for them."

THE TRUE PATHOS: *Youths are normally platonic and virginal in their "boy-girl" relationships.* What a sad irony that "Chastity and Abstinence" courses are needed to reassure students that their natural inclinations are normal.

RHETORICAL QUESTIONS:

1. Were "Chastity and Abstinence" programs ever dreamed of prior to SIECUS-Planned Parenthood school sex programs?
2. Did more than "one in a million" junior or senior high school students engage in sexual intercourse prior to SIECUS-Planned Parenthood's school sex teachings?
3. What percentage of junior and senior high school female students were unmarried and pregnant prior to sex education?

And what percentage of female high school students had abortions prior to sex education?

4. Is Planned Parenthood's propaganda that innumerable students engaged in sex and had abortions by "alley abortionists" prior to Planned Parenthood's abortion services remotely true?

5. What was the delinquency and drop-out rate pre-sex education?

6. How many criminal sexual offenses and rapes were committed daily by high school and college students prior to Planned Parenthood's sex courses? What are these numbers now?

7. How many students used drugs prior to sex education? How many unwed pregnant teenagers committed suicide prior to sex education?

8. How many children engaged in homosexuality, sodomy, oral/genital sex, and other such sexual perversions prior to sex education?

9. How prevalent was preteen and teenage prostitution prior to sex education?

10. How many college dormitories had "in house" prostitutes and pimps prior to Planned Parenthood sex education?

11. How many youths ran away from homes and families prior to sex education?

12. How many thousands of children were permanently stolen from parents to meet the cravings of sexual perverts and the commercial needs of pornographers prior to school sex teachings?

13. How important was idealization and affection in sex relations prior to sex education? How great a part does sexual spiritualization play in today's "sex educated" youths?

Knowingly or unknowingly, even seemingly benign school sex programs act as adjuncts to Planned Parenthood's sexual reformism. For example, "Chastity and Abstinence" school programs help "get off the street" *some* Planned Parenthood's sexually disturbed students making the overall situation appear less ominous.

Before concluding this chapter, at least some small consideration should be given to VIRGINITY.

Psychoanalysis shows repudiation of virginity is a form of social regression, not social progress. Before the current "sexual revolution," 5,000 years of the high value placed on virginity became so evident and so deeply ingrained in the human psyche that it would be difficult for a man or woman to think of a reason explaining: "Why a man should want his fiancee to bring no memory of sex with another man into their marriage."

Psychoanalysis reveals that the first man to have sexual intercourse with a girl or woman leaves a permanent impression in her mind that will *never again* be available to any other man. This phenomenon is referred to psychoanalytically as "enthrallment."

Enthrallment in the female is a "psychical dependency" that occurs irrespective of whether or not the female's first sexual encounter is

- gratifying or disappointing
- pleasurable or painful
- effected by love or hate
- or whatever part the "first man" plays in the female's subsequent life.

A non-virginal woman's relation with her husband is frequently disturbed by recurring enthrallment thoughts involving her first sex partner. These intrusive thoughts cause her to doubt the sincerity of her conjugal love. Her doubts, though delusional, cause feelings of guilt and hypocrisy that all too often play a significant role in short-lived or unhappy marriages.

For these reasons, and many more, virginity clearly remains a virtue.

CHAPTER 2

MOZAMBIQUE SEX

The new hierarchy of sex experts which have developed since the late 1920's largely sanction free love and perversions. Though Freud specifically warned against such dangerous practices, the sexperts not only brazenly misinterpreted and distorted Freud's warnings, but used him to justify their physical sex prescription for relief of all tensions.

Benighted sexperts (among whom may be counted many of today's sex educators, sexologists, psychologists and psychiatrists) contend that physical sex acts comprise the whole of human sexuality, and that sex is strictly a bodily function in the same category as sleeping, breathing, digesting food, etc. According to the sexperts, sex is simply for PLEASURE, and reproduction is only a consequence — not a part of — fornication. However, since all heterosexual genital sex acts include the possibility for reproduction [unless artificial means are taken to avoid it], ones imagination must be truly stretched to believe that in recent years reproduction suddenly degenerated from an integral part of the sex instinct into an accretion.

The "sex is for fun" sex educators and sexologists are unrelenting. They insist that sex and reproduction are only accidentally related. This schizophrenic separation of human sexuality could be dismissed as useless nonsense were it not for the harm done by such sexual skullduggery. Youths are taught that sex is independent of reproduction, and morality. The "sex is for fun" propaganda completely ignores, too, the human need to assuage loneliness thru close loving heterosexual relations between partners who profoundly care for one another.

Loneliness — one of man's earliest, most distressing feelings — can only be allayed by means of a *complete* man/woman union involving a confluence of affectionate and physical sexual currents. Such a union can seldom, if ever, be achieved outside of marriage. Only in marriage are the two sexual components so firmly established that they are heightened, not dissipated, after the sex act. In purely physical sex, completion of the sex act rapidly dissipates affectionate feelings; total sexual needs remain unfulfilled and mental tensions result.

The casual "quickies" between strangers meeting at bars, school classes, cocktail parties, etc. are so devoid of affection that immediately after orgasm, many a sexually overstuffed male complains that the girl sex partner gives him the "Mozambiques". That is, her mere post-coital presence devoid of any affection causes him a feeling of revulsion towards her. He wishes she were as far away from him as possible — Mozambique is the farthest away place known to many young people; thus the boys refer to the unpleasant tensions they feel following meaningless, casual orgastic sex devoid of affection as the "Mozambique Syndrome" [another of today's psychological venereal diseases].

CHAPTER 3

SEX AND THE 10-12 YEAR OLD

Two distinctive psychological features are seen in 10-12 year old preteen children.

The first is an increase in activity associated with the desire for independence, and the second is an increase in activity related to adjusting to adult realities. These increases in psychical energy are referred to as "Thrusts of Activity".

The thrust of activity to be independent follows a similar course in both sexes. But the thrust of activity for adapting to adult reality differs markedly in boys and girls. In girls, the latter thrust of activity is directed inward towards her psyche (mind) and harbingers the female's extraordinary later qualities of:

- intuition (the feminine woman's greatest attribute)
- spiritualization
- empathy
- sensitivity

These natural feminine characteristics are organically determined, that is, they are inborn, and represent the eternal feminine core. To be effective in later life, however, the inherent feminine nature must be encouraged and strengthened throughout prepuberty, puberty, and adolescence.

Modern women all too often resent their inborn feminine qualities — or, to be more correct, *they fear them.* They regard inwardly directed feminine qualities as a form of passivity, inferior to the male's outwardly directed aggressiveness. Such women feel their feminine nature is unobjective, making it difficult for them to compete with and be equal to men.

And indeed, the boy's outward thrust of activity to conquer the realities of his environs gives him an objective aggressiveness which he uses throughout life to master the environment and to achieve utilitarian goals. But it is wrong the claim that the inherent masculine nature is superior or better than inherent feminine characteristics or vice-versa. It is analogous to claiming that air is more important for life than water.

In sexual growth towards adulthood, secrecy and curiosity, which are loosely attached filaments of the human sexual instinct, provide the normal sensual pleasure for 10-12 year old prepubertal children. In girls, sensuality from secrecy and curiosity is shared with another girl — or girls — of the same age. The secrets between the girls primarily involve information regarding physiological sexual processes. The clandestine secrets of prepubertal girls are always discovered independently and individually before they are shared with the girlfriend. Individually acquired sexual knowledge is a major step leading to real adult independence and individualism.

Aside from sensuality derived from secrecy and curiosity, the 10-12 year old girl friendships are non-sexual. Regarding sex, boys play no part in the lives of sexually undisturbed prepubertal girls. (Should sex occur, it is curiosity that usually provokes such action.)

Prepubertal boys [10-12 years old] regard close friendships with girls as a form of effeminacy that should be avoided, and the girls adopt an "I don't care" attitude. School sex education programs severely disturb 10 -12 year old female sexual growth. The sex teachings catapult these children into a world of curt sexual knowledge usurping the independent nature normal for acquiring preteen sexual knowledge. Additionally, the harmless, sensual secrecy pleasures shared by girls of this age are shattered by sex-teachers providing "spoon-fed", sexual knowledge.

The whole framework of prepubertal sexual development is disrupted. Adding to the damage, the pied-piper sex teachers openly or tacitly lead children to regard physical sex as comprising the whole of human sexuality. Children learn to think of sex as an automatic bodily function in the same category as eating, breathing, sweating, etc. The all important mental and spiritual natures of sex are either not emphasized or are disavowed by school sex teachings.

From K - 12, youths are indoctrinated to believe that involvement in sex is necessary if independence and adulthood are to be

achieved. Sex teachers may be sincere and believe in their teachings, but "they know not what they do."

A favorite argument used by proponents of schools "teaching all about sex" is that — "If they don't learn it in school, they'll learn it on the street anyway." The reasoning is as logical as trying to control a fire by pouring fuel on the flames.

There are, indeed, prepubertal and pubertal "street smart" girls who become trapped by their own coquetry — but today's school sex programs are *no way* to help them.

These 11, 12, and 13 year old girls, influenced by the depravity all about them, try to play "grown-up" by practicing their provocative coquetry on the street. Because they realize they have no desire for sexual intercourse, they feel secure. However, when these girls make themselves appear older, or their playful seductiveness becomes too intense, it may release, some men from any scruples they have concerning a juvenile. All too often prepubertal and pubertal children encounter their first sex experience in this way. The first experience frequently is followed by others on the basis of the girl's feeling — "Well, now everything has been lost anyway; what is there to lose?"

Adolescent lesbianism is another ever-increasing school sex education related problem. Students are taught that all sex acts and perversions are normal, simply representing "alternative lifestyles". Given this egregious advice, some disappointed girls, who normally find no sexual gratification in sexual intercourse and feel used and abused by indifferent male partners, turn, once again, to the more sincere girl-to-girl friendships they recall from prepuberty. However, exclusive adolescent female friendships — devoid of boys — tend to lead the girls into "homosexual" feelings. Gradually, erotic impulses turn into homosexual acts. Heterosexual adjustments fail to develop, and the stunted adolescent females remain fixed in homosexual attachments.

When the young girl consults the school psychologist for help because of her fears of becoming lesbian, she is frequently advised: "If you enjoy it, do it."

Mothers and fathers may listen to and see what is going on, but rarely can anyone who attended school prior to the 'sex education

era' begin to fathom the depths to which young people are floundering in non-life-sustaining school learned wanton sex. Numerous scientific studies show that as school sex education programs and school health (sex) clinics increase, there is a corresponding increase in unwed teenage pregnancies, abortions, prostitution, and suicides. Nevertheless, sex education proponents reject all evidence that is contrary to school sex teachings.

Parents must not relinquish their intuitive fears about the effects of school sex education in deference to the theories and opinions of officious educators. Though, perhaps, school officials and teachers are well meaning, their absurd sexual programs are frequently based on:

- statistical questionnaires that are out of sync with real clinical findings
- laboratory gadgeteering
- unsubstantiated personal hypotheses of self appointed sexperts
- etc.

Such methods for evaluating human sexuality all too often provide fallacious conclusions out of touch with reality. The educational system uses such sexual dabblings on children and youths as though they were experimenting with animals.

A parent's sensibilities regarding what is best for sons and daughters are ten thousand times more correct than the opinions of therapist social workers, iconoclastic social scientists, and educators who consider themselves oracles of sexual knowledge.

CHAPTER 4

THE UNWED TEENAGE MOTHER

A considerable number of girls heed the impressions given in sex classes that teenage sex is ordinary and "no big thing". Some reasons given by students for accepting such advice and engaging in anatomical sex are:

(1) to prove to parents and adults that they [the students] are just as independent and grown up as anyone else,

(2) to surpass older siblings and friends and to win prestige by becoming the first in the class to have sexual intercourse,

(3) to take revenge on parents who sex instructors would have students believe are innately puritanical, and hinder youth's need for independence.

The emphasis school sex instructors place on using contraceptives is, paradoxically, one reason many youths fail to use them [to prove themselves independent of adult advice]. Nevertheless, for whatever reasons, an inordinate number of unmarried, preteen and teenage school girls become pregnant. The demands made upon a young girl by pregnancy require that all her mental and physical energies be used for the pregnancy and caring for a newborn child. Little energy is left for personal needs, or for developing her personality which remains incomplete.

Chastity is necessary for the girl to mature completely during adolescence. Premature sexual intercourse can block normal female adolescent maturation; too early a motherhood does the same.

Infantile mothers fail to develop real motherly feelings for their children — even under the most favorable conditions. Additionally, should the father of the unwed girl's child be uncertain, psychological factors usually cause the child to be uncared for, abandoned and in some cases even murdered. The need for a mother to know *who is the father of her child* is intricately connected with motherliness.

The more money government spends to help unwed teenagers, the more these pitiful girls are likely to keep having fatherless babies. Increasing handouts of money is an incentive that offsets the inconveniences of having unwanted, unloved infants.

To slow down this "more babies — more money" merry-go-round, society must develop a social conscience that rejects, rather than helps pay for, such behavior-not to be heartless, but to stop indefatigable unwed females from having imprudent pregnancies for the sake of money.

CHAPTER 5

SEXUAL INSANITY

What is "normal"? The degree of mental health is not determined by absence of inner personal conflicts, but by the way these opposing emotional conditions are reconciled.

"Abnormal" often represents a misrepresentation of what is "normal". Deformed reproductions of normal life are currently being spread by perverted minds, who sick themselves, make the abnormal appear normal. As a physician, I regard any behavior that supports life and allows death to occur from natural causes as normal. Behavior that leads to premature destruction of life is abnormal. The psychological venereal diseases related to today's sex education and the pornographic entertainment media are destructive to life and as such must be considered abnormal.

Sexual morality, which has evolved from mankind's earliest beginnings, helps maintain life. Mature sexuality is associated with sexual morality. The two are antidotes to the death instincts. Nowhere in today's popular school sex programs is life sustaining mature sexuality and sexual morality promoted-though courses on death and suicide are not uncommon.

An uninhibited sex life is contrary to women's inborn feminine nature. The sexually uninhibited woman is an artifact that is produced, sometimes, by a woman's desire to prove herself totally independent or, more frequently, by society's demands imposed upon her. Many of today's sexually aggressive females have turned their backs on the ultimate feminine needs of marriage, family life, motherhood and of loving and being loved. Some "liberated women" attempt to entirely satisfy these loses through copulation. However, these impoverished women derive no profound sensual pleasure from the sex act that can compensate for the feminine needs they have forsaken.

Not only do popular sexual attitudes destroy the lives of many women, but the lives of many men, as well. Some males, who regard free love as a modern day bonanza, aid and abet the state of sexual confusion in today's females. Impressed by sexperts, men and women in the late 20th Century are led to believe the sex act is a cure for all mental tensions.

The argument that the normalcy casual sexual is proven by its prolificacy is as logical as claiming that the bubonic plague in the Fifteenth Century is normal because a great number of people had the disease.

There is one inexorable law in Nature: *"When the sexual instincts are perverted, the death instincts take over."*

The foregoing discourse leads me to believe that the sex teachings of a leading sex education spokesman are grossly abnormal. This spokesman, Albert Ellis, has helped fashion today's school sex programs. Ellis was a main speaker at the *American Association of Sex Educators and Counselors and Therapists* (AASECT) meeting held in Washington, D.C., March 1972. The following excerpts of his AASECT speech are taken from the *Barbara Morris Report,* April 1972:

> "We are now starting planned biology...seeing that certain individuals would better not be born.... Planned biology will plan happiness...having a f—king good time on earth rather than getting into heaven and getting on the right hand of God....
>
> "It is a 'quaint notion' that women have children by their husbands.... We will have sperm banks so we can have Leonardo Da Vincis of our choice.... We may louse up the system and kill ourselves...but we will end up with happier results.
>
> "The goal of most human beings is an ego trip — to show you are a worthwhile human being.... Then they have a heavenly goal — 99 out of 100 have this goal — to be better than others on earth and holier than thou in heaven.... They don't accept humanism — that I will never be anything than human. They have to be taught to be human — f--ked up and human.
>
> "Culture in the future will be based on reality — no spiritual, mystical humanity. If you accept infallible f--ked-up humanity, we will have a better culture and sex education." [Thus spake Albert Ellis.]

In my opinion, Ellis's advice to sex teachers is grossly abnormal. His remark, "We may louse up the system and kill ourselves...but we will end up with happier results," is only half true — the first half.

In 1972, the sensibilities of normal people were appalled by such horrendous recommendations for teaching sex education. But since then our culture has been immersed in an environment rife with pornography and obscenity. To add to the confusion, decisions handed down by courts uphold the "rights" of pornographers and perverts.

Ellis and his followers have managed to persuade a great many people. By their repeated sexual promulgations they have desensitized innumerable minds to sexual schizophrenia. What is normal is no longer generally accepted. And, what is abnormal has become "normal."

Few people can remain totally immune to the incessant bombardment from pornographers, affluent sex educators and aggressive homosexual activists.

> "The avalanche of pornography floods the consciousness with sex to a far greater extent than it should be. It thus deprives the mind of the time and interest needed for other aspects of consciousness, other areas of interest basic to a well-rounded wholesome life. In psychology, this is a problem of "mental hygiene." Sex, a powerful drive, hardly needs any stimulation. It obtrudes itself frequently upon consciousness without outward 'help.' "
>
> Walter Bernard, Ph.D., Asst. Prof. of Psychology,
> Long Island University, from the *New York Times*

psychoanalysis or had misapprehended them.... The doctor's advice to the lady shows clearly in what sense he understands the expression 'sexual life' — namely, in which by sexual needs nothing is meant but the need for coitus or analogous acts producing orgasm and emission of the sexual substances....

"The mental in sexual life should not be overlooked or underestimated. We use the word 'sexuality' in a comprehensive sense.... We have long known that mental absence of satisfaction with all its consequences can exist where there is no lack of normal sexual intercourse.

"Anyone not sharing this view of sexuality has no right to adduce psychoanalytic theses dealing with the importance of the sex act.

"By emphasizing exclusively the physical factor in sexuality, he (the physician) undoubtedly simplified the problem greatly...but he alone must bear the responsibility for what he does....

"No one can ever believe that sexual satisfaction in itself constituted a remedy for the suffering of neurotics...."

Freud's admonitions were effective. Psychiatrists got the message, and psychiatry began making significant advancements up until the 1960's. Then, along came CALDERONE — SIECUS — PLANNED PARENTHOOD. Freud was no longer around to temper them.

Freud's teachings were ignored. Free-love and perversions condoned by SIECUS and Planned Parenthood became fashionable. "Modern" psychiatrists and clinical psychologists began once again to worship the golden calf of physical sex. Sexual hedonistic practices of all kinds were becoming the accepted cure for treating mental disorders.

In the early 1970's, the *American Psychiatric Association* established "psychiatric bloodletting." The leaders of the Association informed its members that henceforth perversions, such as homosexuality, were no longer to be considered mental illnesses. All perversions that were up until this time regarded as ultimate mental sicknesses were now to be considered as normal alternative life styles. SIECUS — Planned Parenthood eagerly supported the declarations of the American Psychiatric Association. (APA, SIECUS, and Planned Parenthood paid no notice to the fact that

CHAPTER 6

PITHY MESSAGES FROM SWEDEN AND RUSSIA

"The sex education promoted by Sex Education Lobbies has existed in Sweden since 1954.

"The King's physician, Dr. Ulf Nordwall, and 140 eminent Swedish doctors and teachers signed a petition to their government expressing concern over sexual hysteria in the young. The petition asserted that this problem appeared to be a product of sex education, and it was now the business of the schools to correct it."

Los Angeles Times, March 1, 1964

It may be of some interest to note, too, that prior to the Russian Revolution, Russian Communists fanatically promoted sex education, free love, pornography and perversion. However, soon after the Communists gained control, they quickly abolished these practices. They seemed to know that no government could endure the destruction of marriage and family. These institutions were rapidly reestablished and virtually sanctified by the Soviet Union. Sex education was put to an end in *1924.*

Why communists and thoughtlessly liberal groups in America insist that carnal sex education, free love, etc. are essential for our democratic society while at the same time they champion Russia's prohibiting such practices is perplexing.

CHAPTER 7

MEDICS AND THE SEXUAL REVOLUTION

From earliest times, Man has faithfully followed the advice of physicians. Long ago, some medicine men decided that trephining (removing a circular section of bone from the skull) was the cure for all medical ailments. This bizarre treatment was considered a primary "therapeutic" procedure, despite the fact that trephining invariably worsened the patient's condition. In some cases, skulls found by archaeologists show one, two, three and frequently more trephinings.

Pity the poor patient or medicine man who dared question the wisdom and intended therapeutic results of medical leaders who recommended boring holes in people's heads. It would have taken a fearless, apolitical "surgeon general" to come forth with the conclusion: "Trephining may be injurious to your health." After killing countless numbers of people, trephining gradually lost its popularity. It was replaced by another treatment that medical leaders then claimed was a sure cure for everything. For centuries, physicians throughout the world were persuaded by affluent medical leaders to rely on this new treatment — bloodletting. Sucking leeches were placed over a sick individual's body or knives were used to cut arteries to drain blood.

Bloodletting became the standard practice for treating malaria, tuberculosis, broken bones, hysteria, etc. Like trephining, bloodletting is responsible for the untimely deaths of countless humans (one of whom was President George Washington). Nevertheless, this practice was used by all physicians blindly following the dictates of their imperious leaders. Woe unto practicing doctors, such as Louis Pasteur, who spoke out disclaiming the rationality of treating patients with blood-sucking leeches. Only by the grace of providence did Pasteur manage to keep his head, much less his medical license. Reluctantly, in the late nineteenth century, some wor medical leaders conceded the errancy of bloodletting. Wh bloodletting lost its popularity, physicians in the early twenti century quickly replaced it with other irrational panaceas. (M: doctors, it seems, have a propensity for quack nostrums.) Calo — a whitish powder consisting of mercurous chloride — becar favorite medicine at the turn of the century. Medical leaders claimed that calomel was useful for treating a multitude of ilr es. The "scientific" rationale given was: "A little mercury poiso won't kill you so, therefore, it must be good for what ails you.

The calomel craze lasted from the late nineteenth century the early 1940's. It was about this time that a new, young me discipline was appearing on the scene — Psychiatry.

Not to be outdone by their trephining, bloodletting, cal prescribing colleagues, psychiatrists of the late nineteent early twentieth century quickly made up their own fa panacea for treating mental illnesses. By thoroughly misinte ing the findings of Dr. Sigmund Freud, early twentieth c psychiatrists proclaimed that anxiety states were due to a sexual intercourse. Treatment, of course, consisted of patients engage in free-wheeling sex practices. Looking fluent leadership to sanction their "new discovery," they attributed their sex treatments to Freud himself.

Stunned by the serious harm that such inane psychiatri was causing, Freud felt compelled to forestall the self-pro sexperts. In 1910, he issued a warning in his artic *Psychoanalysis (The Complete Works of Sigmund Freud — Vol.)* paper, Freud severely criticized psychiatrists who recom free love as a cure all for emotionally distressed patients. C case of one psychiatrist who had advised a woman patient her mental anxieties by engaging in random sexual inter masturbation, Freud said:

"I may do a man who is unknown to me (the physicia injustice by connecting my remarks about *Wild Psychoanalys* this incident. But by so doing I may perhaps prevent other doing harm to their patients....

"The physician was ignorant of a number of scientific theo

the very foundation of psychoanalysis rests on the fact that sexual perversions are the most serious mental illnesses.)

The proclamation of the American Psychiatric Association opened Pandora's Box. Latent homosexuals became blatantly overt. Many young people were converted into becoming homosexuals, and the homosexual population grew by leaps and bounds. Other perverts seemed to come "out of the woodwork." Carnal sex programs were confidently established for children in public schools.

Not only did psychiatrists, clinical psychologists and social workers climb aboard the SIECUS — Planned Parenthood — American Psychiatric Association bandwagon glorifying base sexuality, but physicians in other specialties readily joined in. Uninhibited sex practices seemed to enthrall latter day 20th century medicine men.

By means of illogical excuses, distorted statistics, sophism and other comparable methods, SIECUS — Planned Parenthood — the American Psychiatric Association hurled aside the objections of conscientious, clinically experienced physicians who opposed them. The highly cherished scientific approach that was part of the halcyon years of medicine lasting a few brief years between 1940-1960 was replaced by old "scientific" deceptions and quackery. Acupuncture, megavitamins, meaningless formulas and theories and above all, pagan sexual hedonism make up much of the modern medical armamentaria.

If it weren't for medicines, such as antibiotics and other life-saving pharmaceutical products, and if it were not for the advanced mechanical breakthroughs provided by the manufacturers of technical medical equipment, many of today's medicine men would be at the same scientific level as their brethren of ancient times.

Freudian psychoanalysts provide an oasis of truth for civilized sexual needs. But psychoanalysts have kept a low profile. They seem determined to avoid confrontation with the powerful SIECUS — Planned Parenthood — American Psychiatric Association triumvirate.

Come back Moses! Come back Freud! Physicians are once again worshipping the golden calf of sexual degeneracy, destroying themselves and their followers with Twentieth Century psychiatric bloodletting!

CHAPTER 8

DYNAMICS OF PRETEEN AND TEENAGE SEXUALITY

Polls taken at colleges and universities reveal that 75% of all sexually educated students vote "in favor of unrestrained premarital sexual activities." The results of these polls are contrary to the maxim that — thousands of years of tried and tested, life-sustaining standards and values are *NEVER* improved upon by opinions, and behavior popularized in one or two generations.

Today's sexual attitudes and behavior, into which older as well as younger people have been immersed, are contrary to 150 years of established psychoanalytic facts regarding human sexuality. Popular sexual misinformation is contrary not only to psychoanalytical truths but, also, to Alfred Kinsey's three accurate findings regarding female sexuality. These three, anti-sexual revolution findings derived from his statistical-questionnaire studies are:

- Kinsey's first *clinically confirmed* finding is that the average preteen and teenage girl has an eversion for engaging in sexual intercourse.
- Kinsey's second finding in accord with psychoanalytical observations is that the average female does not experience an orgasm during sexual intercourse before the age of 25-26.
- Thirdly, the average sexually active 30-year old woman has only one or two orgasms per month, regardless of how often she engages in sexual intercourse.

School sex teachings and identifications with sexually uninhibited heroines portrayed in movies and TV shows mislead the public into believing that feminine sexual inhibitions are unnatural and that engaging in casual sex is "chic and normal." Many adolescent girls persuaded by today's sexual school teachings, allow themselves to be used by boys as receptacles for sperm. Some of these girls regret their self disparaging sexual behavior, but, nevertheless, continue sexual offenses against themselves as a form of self-punishment.

Some other females totally reject the sexual impositions made upon them by today's sexual mores and return to their families. Unfortunately, such females are frequently labeled by school sex teachers as "immature" and "family dependent". However, these girls most likely will develop into mature loving wives, excellent mothers and extraordinary homemakers; that is, freaks according to masculinely inclined feminine activists.

Other youthful females give in to the social pressures placed upon them and take on the male's sexual aggressiveness. Many rush hungrily from one man to another and learn to equate love with anatomical sex. Such females keep searching for the "Grand Passion" all their lives — even when they are happily married.

Many female youths learn to use a variety of subconscious mental defense mechanisms to avoid the sexual flummery espoused by the new society. For example, some adolescent girls develop their intellectualism as a means of defense. Unless a girl is born with a surfeit of intellectuality, intellectualism feeds upon the affective life of femininity, leaving the intellectualized female devoid of RICH, FEMININE WARMTH. Other girls turn avidly to excelling in sports, business or professional careers, political or ideological causes, joining communes or cults in subconscious efforts to escape social and peer sexual pressures. However, sports, play, intellectual pursuits, etc. are not adequate substitutes for a close, loving, companionship with a person of the opposite sex.

Prior to school sex education, schools were primary sponsors of comradely, moral groups which allowed youths to express sexual energies through natural platonic relationships. Churches and youth clubs did the same. Since the establishment of schools sex programs, school sponsored sexually moral groups have all but disappeared. Sexually stimulating public discos, immodest home TV shows and today's movies have replaced the former comradely groups which provided teenagers ways to express eroticisms while remaining chaste.

Sexual standards may change, but the inherent life-sustaining needs of human sexuality have not.

Salient Facts of Life that may be worth repeating:
1. School sex courses at all grade levels *can teach one thing only* — and that is physical sex. The vitally important affectionate component of sexuality cannot be learned from a textbook. Furthermore, the emphasis sex education places on physical sex belittles the mental aspect of human sexuality.
2. In the sexual development of prepubertal 10 to 12 year old children, "secrecy and curiosity" provide the only sensual pleasure for this age group.
   - Sex between boys and girls normally plays no part in the lives of prepubertal children.
   - School sex teachings given to 10-12 year olds completely shatter normal sensual secrecy pleasures and compassionate girl-girl friendships. The teachings catapult preteen boys and girls into a world of ready-made sexual information, disrupting this stage of sexual growth.
3. Teenage girls have a **natural aversion to engaging in the sex act**. The girl's erotic feelings are *not* inseparably entwined with sexual intercourse.
   - Contrary to school sex teachings, both sexes in a civilized society...if left undisturbed by school sex teachings — **are normally chaste during puberty and adolescence**.
   - Sexual fantasies and platonic love relationships are the natural means of satisfying male and female eroticisms during adolescence.
   - Sex education encourages students to engage in actual sex rather than fantasies and platonic love relations. The distribution of condoms by their schools give students the impression that "If they are giving us free condoms, they are telling us 'Go ahead and have sex.'"
4. The greatest harm done by school sex education is that all sex courses from K to 12 disrupt natural sex growth.
5. The intrusion of an adult, sex educator or otherwise, into the natural sexual development of children is a form of sexual molestation. The sexual meddlings of educators in sex classes is just as devastating as those of a child molester.
The illiterate sexual intermeddling of sex teachers could ac-

tually be considered *comical*—if it weren't for the terrible harm done to students and society. School sex teachers are truly wanting in understanding the nature of human sexuality. Their assuming the roles of sex educators and sex therapists is sorrowful — and, indeed, not funny.

Instead of advising students to learn from thousands of years of life-sustaining sexual findings, students are taught to rely on the "sex is for fun" transgressions of SIECUS and Planned Parenthood and on the propaganda of homosexual activists.

6. Sexually educated young people are not a new breed of youths, who under the guidance of a progressive educational system, have managed in one generation to improve upon 5,000 years of human sexuality.

7. Preteen-teen students are led to believe it is *normal* and *usual* for youths to engage in sex. To avoid appearing different and rebuffed by classmates, many sex educated girls arrange to lose their virginity by the time they are in junior high school-to whom is relatively unimportant.

8. Perversions are taught as normal, alternative sexual lifestyles. Sodomy is equated with heterosexual genital intercourse. Former U.S. Surgeon General C. Everett Koop, an affluent sex education proponent, states that the human anus is equal to the vagina as a sex organ.

9. The educationists have seemingly been mesmerized by the persistent persuasiveness of the *International Planned Parenthood Federation* and its associates.

   • The educationists' chief reason for teaching children sex is largely based on fatuous sexual suppositions of self-appointed *SIECUS-Planned Parenthood* sexperts. Planned Parenthood's main goal is, apparently, to solve all mankind's problems by:

        (1) sex education
        (2) contraceptives
        (3) abortions
        (4) sterilization

In my opinion, IPPI is banding together with a coterie of ghoulish people whose ultimate aim is to create a "super race" of inhuman homo-sapiens by means of eugenic experiments, euthanasia, tearing apart the cohesiveness of civilized families, and by removing the jurisdiction of parents over their children.

10. The development of the FEMININE WOMAN involves female maturation processes that are not completed until late adolescence.

- Premature sex during adolescence disrupts natural feminine maturation, as does too early a motherhood.
- The demands made upon a young teenage girl by pregnancy require that she use all her energies for the pregnancy and for the caring of a newborn child.
- Infantile mothers fail to develop real motherliness.
- Too early a motherhood does not leave enough psychical energy for developing a girl's personality.

11. To stop the destruction of our civilization, America must reestablish its social conscience.

CHAPTER 9

A CASE IN POINT: THE HINDMARSH MURDERS

A tragic example of the uncontrolled, savage sexual behavior of an adolescent living in an affluent community can be seen in a news article appearing in the June 15, 1985 *Los Angeles Times*:

"Crybaby", 17*, Gets 69 Years to Life
in Two Sex Slayings

By Tim Waters, Times Staff Writer

"...A judge on Friday sentenced a Rancho Palos Verdes teenager to 69 years to life in prison on convictions of sexually molesting and murdering two young girls.

"Superior court Judge Cecil Mills imposed the sentence on Kevin Earl Hindmarsh, who was found guilty last February of the slayings of the 11-year old Palos Verdes Peninsula girls. [Editor's note: on two counts each of murder and sodomy with a foreign object.]

"...After listening to a tearful plea by one of the victim's mothers, that Hindmarsh should be sent to prison, Mills handed down the maximum sentence allowed under law.

"Based on his reading of a psychological report, the judge said he believed Hindmarsh is 'sociopathic'...

"The victims, Neda O'Sullivan and her friend, Kristin Joy Mac-Knight, were found beaten and sexually assaulted in a condominium in the gated Palos Verdes complex where Neda lived with her mother... Neda was already dead. Kristin died the next day at a hospital.

"Defense attorney Fredricks has said that he will appeal the conviction."

*Earl Hindmarsh was probably 14 or 15 when he committed these murders.

The following interpretations are entirely hypothetical. No claim is made as to their accuracy. My aim is only to suggest some explanation for Hindmarsh's behavior.

The area in which Neda O'Sullivan and Kristin Macknight were found murdered was gated. No evidence of forced entry was reported in the *Los Angeles Times* news article. Possibly Hindmarsh was invited into the girl's condominium.

Eleven-year old girls have no desire for the sex act. However, they have a normal sexual curiosity. Neda lived in a California community that was among the first to establish sex education in its schools. A logical inference is that Neda and Kristin attended sex classes which interfered with normal development of their sexual curiosity.

Sexual curiosity in preteen girls is naturally satisfied in private discussions between two girlfriends sharing a close friendship. Direct sexual information provided preteenagers by sex instructors disrupts the preteen stage of sexual growth.

Due to school sex teachings, Neda and Kristin may have been tempted to act out their sexual curiosity with Hindmarsh. Hindmarsh may have become involved in this way.

The school sex programs taken by Hindmarsh during his latency years may have retarded his development for compassion. Additionally, he may have been taught that sodomy and other perversities were simply 'normal variations'. Sodomy and sadism seemed to appeal to Hindmarsh more than sexual intercourse. Tim Waters, in his news report, makes no mention of the girls having been involved in genital sex.

Sex educators regarding sodomy as normal should inform their students that sodomous acts can cause serious infections, hemorrhoids, anal fissures and perforation of the intestinal wall followed by irreversible peritonitis. (The anus is heavily filled with pathogenic bacteria. Puncturing the anus and allowing these infectious organisms to enter the abdominal cavity is always a life threatening situation.)

Though it is difficult to feel sympathy for Hindmarsh, perhaps he should be pitied. He must have had a vestige of compassion in his soul as evidenced by his crying in court, which earned him the name "Crybaby." His crying is an indication he felt some pity — at least for himself.

As previously mentioned, SIECUS — Planned Parenthood sex education would have students believe (1) that young girls relieved of false sexual inhibitions feel unbridled passion for sex, (2) that values and standards depend on enjoying what you do and doing what you enjoy, (3) "Sex is for fun," (4) anal sex acts and all sex acts are normal and equal to genital intercourse.

One can visualize Kevin Earl Hindmarsh seated on his prison cot, thighs up against his chest, chin resting in the palms of his hands while he gazes at the cell wall and ponders: "I meant no harm. I beat them only because they had hang-ups and wouldn't have fun with me. What did I do wrong? Why am I being punished?"

He was simply doing what he had been taught.

Hindmarsh is too far gone to be allowed in everyday society. But what about society accepting carnal sex education and the pornographic media? In my opinion, the latter are probably the primary causes for destroying the lives of Hindmarsh and two eleven-year old girls and for causing interminable grief for the parents of these three young people.

EPILOGUE

The author upholds no claim for the originality of the facts in this book. The information presented is based on established psychoanalytic precepts that have been repeatedly substantiated by real clinical observations. However, psychoanalytic precepts alone were not all that was relied upon. Materials from various sources, other psychological systems and published case histories were used when these stood the acid-test of scientific clinical evaluation and were of value to my patients.

Popular entrancement with data presented by today's sexperts have led many leaders in society to reserve the term "scientific" for data obtained from laboratory gadgeteering, statistical-question-naires and scholasticals. Tremendous weight, often in excess of their importance, is now commonly placed on the findings from such procedures. These methods, when used by institutional professors, academicians and statisticians to learn about human sexuality, produce findings that are usually far removed from sexual truth as it relates to humankind.

For the physician, the quintessence of psychological truth is obtained from the "clinical approach."

The great value of psychoanalysis, which requires a one-to-one relationship between patient and physician, is that it provides insight into the dynamics of human nature and directly attacks the question: "Why do people act that way?"

(Note: There is a *great* difference between psychoanalysis and psychiatry. Psychiatry is basically a descriptive and classifictory science. Its orientation is toward chemical explanations and physical treatments of mental phenomena. Psychoanalysis is a science in which the aim is to understand the dynamics of human behavior; liberally prescribing medications for emotional disorders is not a significant part of psychoanalysis.)

"Psychoanalytic investigation considers the entire mental and emotional nature of humans. It is the only means of acquiring overall information concerning human sexuality.

"Institutional laboratory experiments patterned after bordellos and statistical-questionnaire tests mathematically analyzed are methods used by academician sex experts to measure sexual behavior, motives and feelings. Findings resulting from such investigations all too frequently lead the non-clinical investigators into making erroneous assumptions that are then popularized as scientific truths.*

"The clinical approach to the dynamics of human sexuality involves the whole person. Such study is time-consuming, but through careful observations much insight into human behavior is gained.

"Data accumulated by clinicians is as scientific as that collected by biologists and chemists. There are, however, those who say that psychoanalytic methods are unscientific. To paraphrase psychiatrist Stanley Cobb: 'One need not bother with the intellectual snobs who would keep the term 'science' for laboratory 'gadgeteering.' "[1]

"No book, no journal and no refresher course can teach a doctor so well as the critical study of his own patients."

—I.R. McWhinney
British Medical Journal

No exhaustive bibliography has been added to interrupt the reading of this book. Many authoritative references, however, are quoted.

---

*Consider experiments conducted by Masters, W.A. and Johnson, N.E.

[1]Anchell, Melvin, M.D., A Second Look At Sex Education, Educulture Inc., Publishers, 1972.

APPENDIX

SCHOOL DRUG TEACHERS

A major cause of today's epidemic of student drug users is school drug teachers. Some teachers lead children and young people to use drugs by actual example. Others encourage drug use by openly or tacitly condoning it. The most influential teachers causing students to use drugs — and paradoxically, perhaps, the most innocent — are those convinced that knowledge-based school education programs will correct the problem. The latter instructors conduct drug classes in which detailed information about drugs is given: the street and scientific names of drugs, their colors, feel, chemical makeup, physical and psychical effects, how to use them — everything one could possibly want to know about drugs is taught to students in school drug classes.

Because of ignorance, strong mental resistance, or for other reasons, the knowledge-based drug teachers fail to consider the well established clinical and statistical data that clearly show that "the more students are taught about drugs in school classes, the more students become involved in drug use."

Psychoanalytic clinical observations reveal that when normal young people are instructed about a societal taboo by adult authorities, many youths will be drawn to that activity. About sixty percent of youths have this constitutional compulsion; the remainder have the character to resist that which is prohibited and accept the advice given. Perhaps by doing just the opposite of what adult authorities teach, many young people believe they are proving their independence.

Larry's mother, an intelligent, elegantly attractive woman, sat in my office, tears running down her cheeks. Larry, she said, had been using marijuana for several months and was now smoking it in his room at home. When she rapped on his door and begged him to stop smoking, he flung the door open, cursed her violently, and threw her down the staircase. I was amazed. Larry had been my patient for several years; I knew he loved his mother dearly.

A schedule of one-hour weekly consultations for three months was arranged. Larry kept the appointments gleefully. For three months he joyfully told me about the benefits of marijuana and adjured me to use it myself. There seemed to be no light at the end of Larry's marijuana tunnel.

Suddenly, one day Larry said, "Doc, you're right. I see clearly what you've been saying." Having not said anything for three months, I wondered what he meant. "Yea, Doc, you're right. If everybody — my mom, dad, brother, you, President Reagan — if everybody smoked marijuana, we'd all become like prehistoric cavemen." He continued, "I have an essay to write for English class tomorrow. I'm going to write about how if everybody smoked marijuana, we'd all become cavemen, and get my marijuana smoking classmates to stop."

A week later, Larry returned for his hourly appointment. He stared at me with intense antipathy and spoke with disgust. "It's your fault. You made me write it. My essay was the only one the teacher read out loud, and he made me stand before the front of the class while he read it. When he finished, my teacher said (apparently sardonically, according to the inflection in Larry's voice), 'Tell me, Larry... So what's wrong with the cavemen?' The whole class — my friends — laughed out loud at me." Larry's face turned crimson as he recalled the embarrassment.

Several years later, Larry returned to my office for treatment of a genital infection.

Having not seen him for such a long time, I looked at him for several moments with wonderment. Standing over six feet tall, he was an intelligent, handsome, twenty-two year old man. After graduating from high school, he elected to work for a local manufacturing firm and was now already, one of its junior executives.

He informed me, "I don't use marijuana anymore, but I do use coke."

"I'm not hooked though," he hastened to assure me. "I only use it about three times a week after work."

My gaze fell on his eyes. I saw before me a person for whom life was meaningless. Notwithstanding his success at work, good looks, a bevy of girls, and an heir to much wealth, Larry found no joy in living. Former United States Attorney General Kennedy's son, who killed himself with drugs, came to my mind.

If only Larry's high school teacher had encouraged Larry to stop using marijuana instead of making him appear foolish, Larry's future would be brighter.

My mental restraints against hating human beings may be too highly developed, but, perhaps, there should be another galaxy to which Larry's school drug teacher and other marijuana-coke teacher advocates like him could be sent.

The *only* solution for controlling today's drug problem is for society to once again reestablish its social conscience, abhorring the use and selling of drugs.* Along with a reestablished social conscience, severe laws against drugs must be initiated and enforced.**

Spending taxpayers' money for school drug education programs is throwing good money after bad. Students will be more likely to try drugs. The drug programs will simply make them better informed drug users.

---

* The word, "drug", is used colloquially throughout this paper.

** The current slight lessening of drug use is due to the more firm national stand against drugs, not to knowledge-based school drug teachings.

APPENDIX

PRETEEN AND TEENAGE SEX AND ENVIRONMENTAL INFLUENCES

---

by:

Melvin Anchell, M.D., A.S.P.P.

(American Society of Psychoanalytic Physicians)

Speech given before
XVI International Congress for the Family
Brighton, England
July 12-15, 1990

Copyright 1990

Reprinted by: THE HOFFMAN CENTER
Education for the Family
5266 Citizens Parkway
Selma, AL 36701
(205) 872-3851
Bobbie Ames, Administrator

Thank you for your kind introduction, and good afternoon everyone.

The topic of my talk is a psychoanalytic look at some environmental influences — *especially school sex education* — that effect preteen and teenage sexual behavior.

The facts to be presented are based on:

1) Established psychoanalytic principles,
2) My personal observations of young patients whom I have treated psychoanalytically,
3) Case histories of other clinical investigators, and
4) Any source of data that can be clinically substantiated with everyday patients.

I will be careful to speak as a psychoanalyst, and only on matters in which I have expert knowledge.

My discussion will first consider some environmental influences affecting 10-12 year old sexual behavior and will follow with the effect of these same influences on the sexual behavior of pubertal and adolescent youths.

A distinctive characteristic seen in 10-12 year old children is an increase in activity to adjust to the realities of the adult world. This increase in activity in 10-12 year olds to adapt to grown up realities differs markedly in boys and girls. In the boy, his adaptations to adult realities are directed outward, towards his environs, giving him an objective aggressiveness which the male uses throughout life to master the environment and to achieve utilitarian goals. In girls, their increased activity to become grown-up is directed inward, towards the psyche, that is, their minds.

This "inward" direction of young girls' adaptations to adult reality harbingers the female's later ability to understand and grasp life through her extraordinary feminine capacity for:

1) Sensitivity
2) Subjectivity
3) Spirituality
4) Empathy, and
5) Intuition.

These remarkable feminine qualities are inborn and represent the "eternal core" of the feminine woman. However, to be effective in later life, the feminine nature must be strengthened throughout puberty and adolescence.

Prepubertal boys' and girls' activities brought about by the desire to be independent and grown are greatly influenced by (1) identifications with parents, and (2) by consciences instilled in the minds of young people by parents. However, when the 10-12 year old reaches the age of 13, that is, puberty, psychological changes occur which push parental influences into the background, and identification with individuals outside the home begin to play major roles in influencing the behavior of teenagers. If environmental influences are in accord with previous parental teachings, new adaptations to life are made harmoniously, and pubertal-adolescent maturation progresses smoothly into early adulthood. When, however, the environment is *out of sync* with parental teachings, parents and the child's conscience are rapidly deprecated in the minds of most youths. Under such circumstances, leaders in the contravening environment replace the authority of parents, and the consciences of young people are decimated by the beliefs and teachings of the new leaders.

In the sexual development of 10-12 year old children, secrecy and curiosity, which are loosely attached filaments of the human sexual instinct, provide the sensual pleasures normal for this age group. In girls, sensual gratification derived from secrecy and curiosity is shared with other girls of the same age. The clandestine secrets of prepubertal girls are always investigated privately before sharing the findings with a girlfriend. The privacy used in acquiring sexual information is a first step in life leading to individuality and independence.

Pleasures derived from sharing secrets with other girls are the only "prepubertal sensual activity." In all other respects, the 10-12 year old girl friendships are normally non-sexual. The privately investigated secrets concern physiological sexual matters and are not related to sex with boys. Sex between girls and boys normally plays no part in the lives of 10-12 year old children. Prepubertal boys regard close friendships with girls as unmanly, and girls adopt an "I don't care" attitude.

Today's school sex education given to prepubertal children completely shatters normal sexual secrecy pleasures and compassionate girl friendships by catapulting 10-12 year olds into a world of ready-made, instant sexual information. Such school interferences usurp girl-to-girl friendships with their harmless sensual secrets, and at the same time disrupt the beginning development of individualism and independence.

Many acts of gangsterism, prostitution and criminality in 10-12 year old children result from the violent interruption of normal pre-teen sexual growth with premature sex acts foisted by school sex teachings. Since the advent of school sex education, promiscuity, pregnancies and venereal diseases are no longer uncommon in 10-12 year old children.

Almost invariably pubertal and teen youths confused by family and environmental differences will develop, in some degree, attitudes offensive to the family. For example, youths brought up in sexually moral homes become critical of the family when school sex courses glorify all types of physical sex while at the same time "damning by faint praise" the affectionate nature of human sexuality and *the glorification of the sex partner* stressed by parents.

School sex courses at all grade levels *can teach one thing only*, and that is physical sex. The vitally important, life-sustaining affectionate component of human sexuality cannot be learned from a school textbook. It is absolutely impossible.

Unfortunately, notwithstanding family allegiances, teenagers all too often favor the school sex teachings, and as a result it is virtually impossible for them to make sexually mature adjustments in later life.

[I should stop here for a moment to make perfectly clear that statements and conclusions in this discussion refer to SIECUS-Planned Parenthood type sex education established in 80% of schools in the United States. However, it would be reasonable to assume that (1) because of the close ties between England and the United States, and (2) because of the overwhelming worldwide influence of the International Planned Parenthood Federation, sex teaching in English schools under the guidance of your *Family Planning Association* are most likely mirror images of the school sex programs in the United States.]

But to continue, by the age of 13 prepubertal girl-to-girl friendships gradually lessen as the girls grow older and go their separate ways. Puberty is also a time when sexual energies that have remained dormant during the latency years of 6-12 are once again reawakened. The reawakened sexual energies in pubertal boys are direct and are centered in the male genitalia. The reawakened eroticisms of the 13-year old girls follow a MUCH different course.

Because teenage female biological and psychological maturations are not completed until late adolescence, and because the female genitalia remains anesthetic to anatomical sex until the average age of 25 to 26, nature has provided the young girl with a natural aversion to the sex act. Contrary to the teachings of sex educators, both sexes — if left undisturbed by school sex teachings and the pornographically-oriented entertainment media — are normally chaste during puberty and adolescence.

Though the teenage girl has a natural aversion to engaging in the sex act, her sexual desires, however, may be as intense as the boy's. Teenage female eroticisms involve: (1) the desire to love and to be loved, (2) kisses and caresses, (3) tender words of love, (4) sexual fantasies, and (5) sometimes thoughts of pregnancy and motherhood — but unlike the male, the girl's sexual eroticisms are not inseparably entwined with the sex act.

The dichotomy between the adolescent boy's capability for the sex act and the girl's natural reluctance to sexual intercourse may seem strange, but Nature always has a reason for what it does. The teenage girl's reluctance to the sex act serves to strengthen the affectionate and spiritual nature of sex. Through affection and sexual spiritualization, both sexes learn to regard sex and the sex partner with the utmost importance.

Spiritualization of sex leads to the idealization of members of the opposite sex. Idealization of a special someone makes life complete. The answer is not that 1 plus 1 equals 2, but that 1/2 plus 1/2 make *one whole person.* This is the basis for monogamous love which forms the foundation for Western Civilization.

It should be noted that sexual fantasies are important for adolescent sexual development. The fantasies primarily consist of an ardent desire for sensual love with someone of the opposite sex. Such fantasies are (1) natural, (2) beneficial, and (3) gratifying, but they are not meant to be carried out in real life.

Unfortunately, classroom sex instructions are an anathema to adolescent fantasies. School sex teachings suppress sensual fantasy life by encouraging students to engage directly in sex acts. For example, many Planned Parenthood sex teachers place condoms in Valentine greeting cards and send these cards to students with the wish for a Happy Valentine's Day. The only admonition given to students is that before engaging in sex, they should use multi-colored, multi-flavored condoms freely distributed by school-based sex clinics. To paraphrase the impression of many sexually educated youths: "If they are teaching it to us in school, they are telling us to go ahead and have sex — for what other reason are they giving out free condoms?"

It should be clearly understood that under usual normal environmental conditions, teenagers are normally chaste, preferring to engage in platonic relationships. Some reasons given by youths for becoming sexually active in today's world are:

1) To prove that they are grown-ups
2) To surpass older siblings and friends
3) To gain prestige from classmates by engaging in   school condoned sex
4) To take revenge on parents who are accused of thwarting independence, and
5) To take advantage of the sexual permissiveness overlooked by schools.

Another school sex education related catastrophe is the ever-increasing numbers of adolescent lesbians in the United States. Students in sex classes are taught that all perversions are normal. Given this assurance, some disappointed girls, who find no gratification in genital intercourse, and feel they have been used and abused by providing indifferent males with sexual satisfaction, turn once again to the more earnest girl-to-girl friendships they recall from prepubertal years. However, exclusive relationships between adolescent girls differ from the 10-12 year old girl friendships. Erotic feelings are more intense during adolescence, and may push 13-21 year old girls devoid of male companionship into homosexual activities which arrest further heterosexual development.

The greatest harm done by today's school sex education is that all sex courses, from kindergarten through high school, destroy natural sexual growth. In humans, unlike any other creatures, three phases of sexual development occur before adult sexual maturity is reached: the first phase of human sexual development occurs at birth and lasts through the fifth year of life; the second phase begins at six and continues through the age of twelve; and the third phase of human sexual development starts in puberty around the age of thirteen, and is not completed until late adolescence.

Though time does not permit explaining how and why, school

sex teachings at all grade levels disrupt sexual growth during the three phases of human sexual development. The fact is that the intrusion of an adult — whether a sex teacher or not — into the sexuality of children is a form of child molestation that can be just as harmful as an actual attack by a child molester.

Sex education proponents are resolute in their resolve to involve themselves in the sexual development of children and young people, and to inculcate physical sexual matters into youths' minds. The illiterate sexual intermeddlings of sex teachers in the developing sexuality of children and youths could actually be considered *comical* if it weren't for the egregious harm that is done to students and society.

The sex "educators" have no compunction in overriding any data that is not supportive of their sex education theories. For example, a recent international survey on approximately 30,000 thirteen year old students from a number of nations clearly showed — and I quote: "American students come out at the bottom of the heap scholastically...and revealed a marked weakness in higher order thinking skills..." Such research is disregarded by sex educators who insist that "immature juvenile students" formulate new sexual standards and values and use their own judgment in determining whether or not to engage in sex — and if so, what sex acts to commit.

In developing new standards and values, the students are implicitly or openly cautioned not to heed thousands of years of tried and tested, life sustaining findings, nor pay attention to teachings of parents, because these sources — students are made to believe — are prejudiced, puritanical, outdated, and erroneous. Instead, students are taught to rely on the "sex is for fun" transgressions of Planned Parenthood, and on the sexual propaganda of homosexual activists.

Sexually educated young people are not a new breed of youths who, under the guiding patronage of a progressive educational system, have managed in one generation to change five thousand years of human sexuality. The new breed simply represents misled children who have been rushed into "SHAM SEX" by benighted sex educators. Parents and the public may listen and even see, but rarely can anyone who attended school prior to today's sex education possibly fathom, how deeply sex-educated young people have been led into wanton sex. For example, recently a major Chicago newspaper casually reported that 80% of freshmen to senior female students in a Chicago high school are pregnant. Can any parent over thirty truly imagine what is happening in education to create such disasters?

By some means or other, sex teachers in the United States, under the auspices of SIECUS and Planned Parenthood, have summarily seized the right to teach children and youths...

1) How to mate in every which way
2) How to override inborn mental barriers against perversions,
3) How to rely on contraceptives and abortions
4) And how to engage in all sex acts without guilt...obviously these are the characteristics of pimps and prostitutes.

To justify their coup, educators frequently use the argument that parents don't feel comfortable teaching sex to children and prefer leaving such matters to school teachers. At the same time, some teachers complain that they are being imposed upon by parents — especially those parents who expect schools to uphold Judeo-Christian sexual morality. A morality, incidentally, that

1) supports the struggle for existence
2) sustains civilized lives
3) is in line with all enduring religions, and
4) a morality whose life-sustaining nature is substantiated by repeated psychoanalytic observations.

At no time do educators remotely explain who decided, and for what reason, it suddenly became fashionable to teach physical sex and perversions to school children living in the late 20th century!

Aside from evading these questions, sex educators shun the most fundamental psychoanalytical facts that unequivocally show school sex education from kindergarten to 12 causes irreparable harm to students throughout life. For example, when the psychoanalytic fact became widely known that sex education destroys sexual growth and personal development during the latency years of six to twelve, Mary Calderone, the leader of

SIECUS, simply decreed that the Latency Period in six to twelve year old children did not exist. Subsequently, followers of *SIECUS* and *Planned Parenthood* dismissed from further consideration the pernicious harm done to six to twelve year old children by school sex teachings.

Not only do sex educators disregard scientific psychoanalytic knowledge, but when it suits their purpose, they likewise turn their backs to the findings of their *very own* principal sex investigators. For example, Alfred Kinsey is one of the sex educators "leading lights." In his sex questionnaire studies, Kinsey found and reported that the average teenage female had an intense aversion for engaging in the sex act. Nevertheless, his finding is rejected by sex educators, and students in sex classes are taught that it is usual and gratifying for young girls to engage in sexual intercourse. To avoid appearing abnormal and rebuffed by their classmates, many female students arrange to lose their virginity to someone when they become fourteen.

Another "guiding light" sexologist highly regarded by *Planned Parenthood* sex educators is Dr. William Masters. SIECUS's Mary Calderone virtually deified Masters for his sexual experiments in which he used prostitutes, as well as paid and unpaid volunteers. Recently, however, Dr. Masters must have had a change of heart, for he denounced homosexuality and homosexual sex acts in a magazine article.

Here again, however, the educators ignore the teachings of their chief authorities. Homosexuality, more than ever, is still taught in schools as a normal, sexual life style; and homosexual acts, such as sodomy, are regarded as entirely equivalent to heterosexual genital intercourse. The recent U.S. Surgeon General, C. Everett Koop, M.D. — a powerful sex education proponent — openly states that the human anus is equal to the vagina as a sex organ.

Educationists have seemingly been mesmerized by the persistent persuasiveness of *International Planned Parenthood Federation* and its associates. The educationists' reasons for teaching children and young people sex are based on frequently fatuous, statistical questionnaires, laboratory gadgeteering, and the sexual suppositions of self-appointed SIECUS-Planned Parenthood sexperts.

Planned Parenthood seems fanatically convinced that the solution to all of mankind's problems is to control world population by means of contraceptive abortions, and sterilizations. Slowly but surely human eugenics, euthanasia, and destruction of traditional family relationships are being added to Planned Parenthood's goals. (Excuse my curtness, but such aims, at best, are inhuman and delusional.)

An ostentatious cliche used by proponents of school sex education is: "If they don't learn it in school, they'll learn it on the street anyway." Such justification for teaching children *carnality* is as logical as trying to control a fire by dumping more fuel on the flames.

It is true, that there are "street smart" pubertal girls who, not infrequently became trapped into sex acts by identifying with sexually loose older females and by emulating sexually uninhibited heroines seen in many of today's movies and television shows. *But* sex education is *not* the solution for these young girls who play out their provocative coquetry on the street and who feel secure because they realize they have no real desire for sexual intercourse. However, when their seductive coquetishness becomes too intense, it may free some men from any scruples they have concerning a juvenile In this way, all too often, 12, 13, and 14-year old girls, who frequently make themselves look older, encounter their first sex experience. The first experience is, not infrequently, followed by others on the basis of the girl's feeling... "Well, now everything has been lost anyhow — what is there to lose?"

Some sexually active girls regret their sexual involvements, but, nevertheless, continue sexual offenses against themselves as a form of self-punishment. Prostitution, venereal diseases, and illegitimate children are frequent consequences of their remorse.

A generally known psychoanalytic fact concerning human sexuality is that the female is prone to follow the conventions of her culture. If her social order regards chastity as a virtue, she becomes chaste. If her society espouses free love, she may readily assume the characteristics of a loose woman.

The brusque truth is that today's sexually emancipated female is not an example of new progressive social changes which have made her a free individual. She simply represents a woman — or girl — who has become a slave to the demands of her society. Some girls resist this sexual enslavement by returning to their families. Sex school teachers frequently label such girls as "immature and family dependent," but in reality these chaste young females develop into fully mature women who become ideal spouses, mothers, and homemakers.

Conversely, some other girls accept the sexual expectations society makes upon them and take on the characteristics of the male's sexual aggressiveness. Many rush hungrily from one man to another and learn to equate love with fornication. Such females keep searching for the "Grand Passion" all their lives — even when they are happily married.

A variety of subconscious defense mechanisms are used by many modern females to fend off the sexual flummery imposed upon them. For example, some girls turn to intellectualism as a means of defense. This particular defense reaction against sexual impositions may seem sound, but, unfortunately, intellectualism — unless the girl is born with a surfeit of intellectuality — feeds upon the affective life of femininity. That is, a girl's intellectualism or objectivism gets much of its energy from female emotions, leaving her largely depleted of rich, warm, feminine feelings.

Other defense reactions against unwanted anatomical sex can be seen in girls who

1) excel in sports, or who
2) take up professions and business careers, or who
3) become activists in various ideological or political groups, or who
4) join communes or cults as a means of escape.

However, sports, play, work, and intellectual pursuits are *not* adequate substitutes for a close, emotional relationship with a person of the opposite sex.

Planned Parenthood, militant feminists, and homosexual activists will regard the various subconscious defense mechanisms used by "1990 females" to keep from engaging in uninhibited sex as grand achievements. Many Planned Parenthood advocates and school change agents will argue that the very proclivity of feminine "tricks" used to circumvent sexual involvements is proof positive that the masculinized woman is inherently normal. Eons of feminine traits in women, they contend, are a result of human subjugations that the current champions for masculinizing women have fought long and hard to quixotically remove.

However, not because of social subjugations, but because of biological, anatomical, and psychical reasons, woman's more inhibited sexual life cannot be equated to man's. The fact is that certain highly developed basic, inborn sexual inhibitions in women are not found to such a degree in men. Woman's normally heightened sexual inhibitions give rise to her valuable emotions and spiritualized eroticism. Without these qualities, the usual female reaction to sexual intercourse remains disappointing and empty. Natural feminine sexual restraints intensify woman's sexuality and enriches her entire mental and physical sexual life.

It is true, however, that the feminine woman is, indeed, highly erotic. But there must be a harmonious interplay between her eroticism and her femininity. Without recounting detailed psychoanalytic explanations, it can be unequivocally said that the uninhibited woman readily yielding to sexual intercourse without becoming entangled in mental conflicts [as well as sexually transmitted diseases] is found only in current fiction written largely by sexually unenlightened or discreditable men — or homosexuals.

In any regard, proclivity is not the acid test for life-sustaining values and truths. If 50 million people engage in sexual destructiveness, what they do is still destructive.

The trouble with the sexual philosophies of Planned Parenthood, feminist activists, and homosexuals is that their theories do not work. Though human bodies may perform according to the bizarre philosophies of sexperts, the human mind cannot.

To sexually love a woman and not respect or appreciate her inner emotional nature is to treat her as a domesticated bovine animal. Pitiably, many present generation females accept this status largely because of the brainwashings of Planned Parenthood, school sex education, and the pornographic entertainment media. More pitiably, some females are not only accepting this status but are helping to promote it.

The goal of a boy should be to become a man and that of a girl to become a woman. The development of the feminine woman —("God's greatest gift to humanity") — involves female maturation processes that are not completed until late adolescence. Premature sex during adolescence disrupts natural feminine maturation, as does "too early a motherhood." The demands made upon a young teenage girl by pregnancy require that she use all her energies for the caring of a newborn child.

Infantile mothers fail to develop real motherliness, even under the most favorable conditions; and a too early motherhood leaves little psychical energy for developing the girl's personality which remains incomplete.

In humans, unlike animals, when affectionate needs are not met and physical sex is all that remains, sex becomes meaningless and life becomes empty. This psychoanalytic maxim is readily apparent in the suicides of sexually educated, sexually active youths. Suicide now ranks as the leading cause of death in young people under the age of 21 in the United States.

Over the past 25 or so years, a sexual revolution has been destroying Western Civilization by vilifying human sexuality. The effects have been truly devastating. Assuming this scourge has not, as yet, brought us to the point of no return, WHAT CAN BE DONE?

First, I believe, society must re-establish its social conscience, a conscience that — as just a generation or so ago —

1) will not sanction free love and perversions
2) will not permit gutter sex to be spread publicly by a pornographically oriented entertainment media
3) and a social conscience that will not tolerate schools acting as child molesters.

Sexual revolutionists, by corrupting the meaning of "free speech" and by stretching the boundaries of sexual indecency, are persuading much of the public into accepting social degeneracy. Fortunately, however, civilization is not a one way street. Restoration of a social conscience can:

1) stop the decline of our civilization and

2) help it climb back out of the abyss into which it has been flung by those determined to make Western Society a bastille for pagan sexual hedonism.

In conclusion, two matters stand out: First, life sustaining sex completely depends on an affectionate, monogamous, man/woman, long lasting, love relationship. Such relationships are essential for the survival of civilizations based on families composed of individuals living by consciences, instead of barbarians living by instincts only. And secondly, for the benefit of all mankind, it is just as important to eradicate the *psychological venereal diseases* that are rife today, as it is to eradicate physical venereal diseases, such as AIDS. Both arise from the malignant abuse of human sexuality.

Thank you for your kind attention and for inviting me to visit England and to participate in your meeting.